B-17
FLYING FORTRESS

in detail & scale

Part 1

Alwyn T. Lloyd
Terry D. Moore

KALMBACH BOOKS

Airlife Publishing Ltd.
England

CONTRIBUTORS:

Bert Kinzey	Terry Smith
Dan Bell	Gerald Hasselwinder
Steve Birdsall	Bill Slatton
Peter M. Bowers	David W. Menard
Lonna Brooks	Marilyn A. Phipps
Walter J. Boyne	Victor D. Seely
James Bethards	Gordon S. Williams
Chuck Harney	Byron L. Wingett
Roger Harney	Harry Gann
Robert Ferguson	Joseph Harlick
Lloyd S. Jones	Monogram Models, Inc.
Frederick Johnsen	Revell, Inc.
J. Weimer	

U.S. Air Force Museum, Wright Patterson AFB.
1361st Audio Visual Squadron (MAC)
The Boeing Company Historical Services and Public Relations Departments

FIRST EDITION
FIFTH PRINTING

First Published in Great Britain by

Airlife Publishing Ltd.
7 St. John's Hill
Shrewsbury, SY1 1JE

Lloyd, Alwyn T. & Moore, Terry D.
B-17 Flying Fortress in detail and scale.
Part 1—Production Versions
1. B-17 bomber
I. Title II. Series
623.74'63 TL 685.3
ISBN 0-85368-500-2 UK

Front Cover: B-17C taking off from Boeing Field. (Boeing Photo K-8).

Rear Cover: B-17B at Boeing Field. Note tail light, rudder, and crew door details. (Boeing Photo)

B-17 G-5-VE fuselage being moved to receive its wings. *(Lockheed-Vega C5156)*

INTRODUCTION

Each book in the Detail & Scale Series requires numerous photographs that show detailed close-ups of the aircraft both inside and out. Obtaining these photographs for an aircraft that is in operational service usually means a lot of coordinating with the "right people" in order to gain access to the ramp and the aircraft. But detail photos are always harder to get than general shots or photographs of markings. You have to find someone willing to open cockpits, radars, access panels, and other parts of the aircraft.

If getting the detailed photos is difficult for an operational aircraft, it is even worse for an aircraft that is no longer in service. Most photographers don't emphasize detail photographs, or are unable to get them. Therefore, even if an older photo collection is located, few, if any detail shots can be found. Restored aircraft may be available, but they usually are not accurate as far as details are concerned. This is particularly true of combat aircraft that no longer have their armament and other equipment.

About the only two places left to look are in the files of the company that built the aircraft, or in the archives of the country or military service that operated it. It is amazing and disappointing how even these sources are now discarding some of their one-of-a-kind photographs because of a lack of space.

Al Lloyd has been able to find rare and extensive detailed coverage of the B-17 in Boeing's files. Most of these detailed photographs have never before been published, and they are as clear and sharp as if they had been taken yesterday. Some of the general photographs show their age a bit, but these too usually are the best photographs of the B-17 that are available today.

In order to give this famous aircraft the coverage it deserves, Detail & Scale will present the B-17 in two parts. This book will cover the production versions of the B-17, and later, part two will cover the special versions and adaptations.

We are indeed pleased to be able to present this book, which is our first on a WW II aircraft. It is our belief that the following pages contain the most detailed coverage of the B-17 ever published.
Bert Kinzey
President, Detail & Scale, Inc.

THE FLYING FORTRESS

Model 299 prototype, with civil registration number X13372 on wing, taxis across Boeing Field.(Boeing 8240)

In May, 1934, the U.S. Army Air Corps issued Air Corps Circular 35-26 which announced a competition for a new multi-engined bomber. All entrants had to be built and flown to Wright Field, Ohio for evaluation in late 1935. Additionally, each entrant was to be purely a speculative venture by the manufacturer, since only the winner would receive compensation.

In those days the term "multi-engine" was construed to mean a twin-engined aircraft, but Boeing opted for a four-engine design. This design, designated Model 299 by Boeing, combined the features of the Model 247 commercial transport and the yet unbuilt XBLR-1 (XB-15). The basic construction of the Model 299 was based on the Model 247, while the engine arrangement, fuselage cross-section, and military crew and equipment distribution paralleled the XB-15. In size, the Model 299 was mid-way between the Model 247 and the XB-15.

Preliminary design on the Model 299 began on June 18, 1934, and construction commenced on August 16, 1934. Final design started in April, 1935, and the aircraft was rolled out on July 17. The first flight was made on July 28, 1935. By August 20, the aircraft was ready for competition, and was flown from Seattle to Wright Field. On this flight the 299 averaged 252 miles per hour, setting a non-stop record for the distance of 2,100 miles. At that time it was the largest landplane in the United States. However, it soon lost this distinction to the XB-15 when that aircraft was built.

During testing at Wright Field, the 299 technically belonged to Boeing and not to the Air Corps. Therefore it carried the civilian registration number X13372. Early testing was very promising, but on

October 30, 1935 the aircraft was lost in a crash. The cause of the crash was an unremoved elevator control lock. To prevent the same thing from happening again, the first formal written checklist was devised, and since then such checklists have become standard for almost every aircraft flying.

Fortunately, the Air Corps had been impressed enough with the 299 before the crash to award Boeing the contract and order thirteen more aircraft designated Y1B-17. The name "Flying Fortress" was given by a newspaper reporter covering the rollout ceremonies. The B-17 "Flying Fortress" was born!

THE B-17 DESCRIBED

Between the Model 299 and the last B-17G, the "Flying Fortress" underwent many changes. However, the construction and layout remained basically the same for all versions. Presented here is a basic description of the B-17 design.

Structure:

The aluminum structure of the B-17 was designed within the state-of-the-art using lessons learned with the Model 247. Basically, the airplane was a combination of a light formed sheet metal framework with a thin skin forming a rigid structure.

Fuselage:

A conventional all-metal, semi-monocoque design was employed in the fuselage. The basic construction was circular with a raised addition for the cockpit and radio compartment. A series of vertical bulkheads and circumferential frames connected with longitudinal stringers and covered with stressed skin comprised the basic fuselage structure. Entrance to the fuselage could be gained through the crew access hatch in left side of the fuselage forward of the wing or through the crew entry door located on the right side of the fuselage. Prior to the B-17E the door was located immediately aft of the wing, while the later aircraft had the door moved further aft to a position just forward of the horizontal stabilizer. In general the window cutouts in the structure remained the same throughout the life of the airplane series; however, major differences in the cutouts did occur to meet the changing armament configurations.

Wings:

The wings were made up of four major assemblies. A pair of inboard wing panels supported the nacelles, main landing gear, and flaps. A set of twelve taper pins were used to join each inboard wing assembly to the fuselage. Each outboard wing panel was joined to its mating inboard wing panel by a set of thirteen taper pins. The wing front and rear spar trusses were made up of bolted and riveted square cross-sectioned tubing. Tube and channel trusses made up the ribs, and reinforcement for a corrogated inner skin was employed on the wings. A symmetrical NACA airfoil was employed, and fabric covered ailerons were installed on the outer wing panels.

Empennage:

The tail surfaces consisted of cantilevered vertical and horizontal stabilizers. Sheet metal covered the stabilizers, while fabric was employed on the rudder and elevators.

Systems:

Ailerons, elevators, and a rudder comprised the primary flight control surfaces, and each surface had a trim tab. These controls were operated by means of unboosted cable systems. An innovation on the B-17Gs was the formation stick which offered an electric power boost to the control column. The wing flaps were electrically operated via a series of torque tubes mounted behind the wing rear spar. Manual extension could be accomplished by means of a crank located in the radio compartment.

Another innovation on the B-17 were the Hamilton Standard hydromatic constant speed pro-

pellers. Later versions of the B-17 had full-feathering propellers. The propeller/engine combination resulted in an extremely quiet airplane despite its size.

The airplane fuel system grew to meet service requirements. Initially six tanks within the inboard wings comprised the fuel storage capability of the B-17. A tank situated between the engines and aft of the front spar provided fuel for the outboard engine. A second tank was located inboard of the inboard engine, between the front and rear spars, and served the inboard engine. A feeder tank was located between the tank for the outboard engine and the rear spar, and together these tanks held a total of 1700 gallons. Beginning with the B-17B additional fuel could be carried in a pair of dropable bomb bay tanks which added another 820 gallons to the fuel capacity. The B-17F's fuel capacity was further increased with the addition of tanks in the outboard wing panels which were known as "Tokyo tanks."

Landing Gear:

The landing gear was electrically operated by a toggle switch located on the pilot's central control panel immediately ahead of the engine control stand. This switch was adjacent to the electric flap control switch, and it was possible to retract the landing gear instead of the flaps when the aircraft was on the ground. (Long after the B-17, aircraft designs incorporated human engineered controls with a flap-shaped flap control handle and a wheel-shaped landing gear control handle.) A manual gear extension could be accomplished by use of a crank inserted in a fitting located on the aft face of the forward bulkhead in the bomb bay. Each main gear had to be operated separately. The tail wheel could also be manually operated by means of a crank located on a bulkhead in the rear of the airplane.

B-17 Firsts:

The Model 299 was the first American airplane to have air brakes in the landing gear wells, and the first to be equipped with flaps on the rear edges of its wings to serve as air brakes in landing.

On the pages that follow are what we believe to be the most extensive photographic coverage in a single publication of the production versions of the B-17 and the aircraft that led to its design and development. In each section are photographs and captions that cover the major changes that the B-17 design underwent as it progressed from the Model 299 thru the B-17G.

MODEL 247

Model 247. The influence that this aircraft had on the design of the B-17 is clear in this photo.

(Boeing K33363)

The Boeing Model 247 design formula was a significant influence on the design of the B-17 as well as on the designs of many future transport aircraft. It was the first all-metal streamlined monoplane transport, and was officially classified by Boeing as a "twelve-place, landplane monoplane, closed cabin, low wing, twin engine" aircraft. It first flew on February 8, 1933, and featured retractable landing gear, an automatic pilot, trim tabs, and deicing equipment. Several were drafted into Army service for transport and training duties as C-73, but the major user was United Air Lines, with Boeing Air Transport, National, and Varney also using the aircraft. It was powered by two Pratt and Whitney S1D1 Wasp engines of 550 horsepower. These engines were supercharged, which was a first for a transport type aircraft. Formerly only military aircraft had superchargers. It was also said that the Model 247 was the first production transport to have complete interchangeability of all main parts, one plane with another. A total of seventy-five 247, 247A, and 247D aircraft were built.

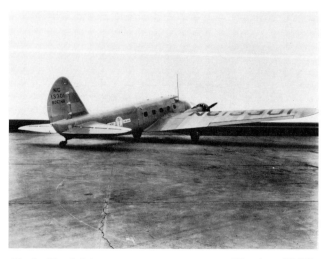

Early Model 247.   *(Boeing 6112)*

Model 247 cockpit.   *(Boeing 6245B)*

MODEL 247
1/144th SCALE

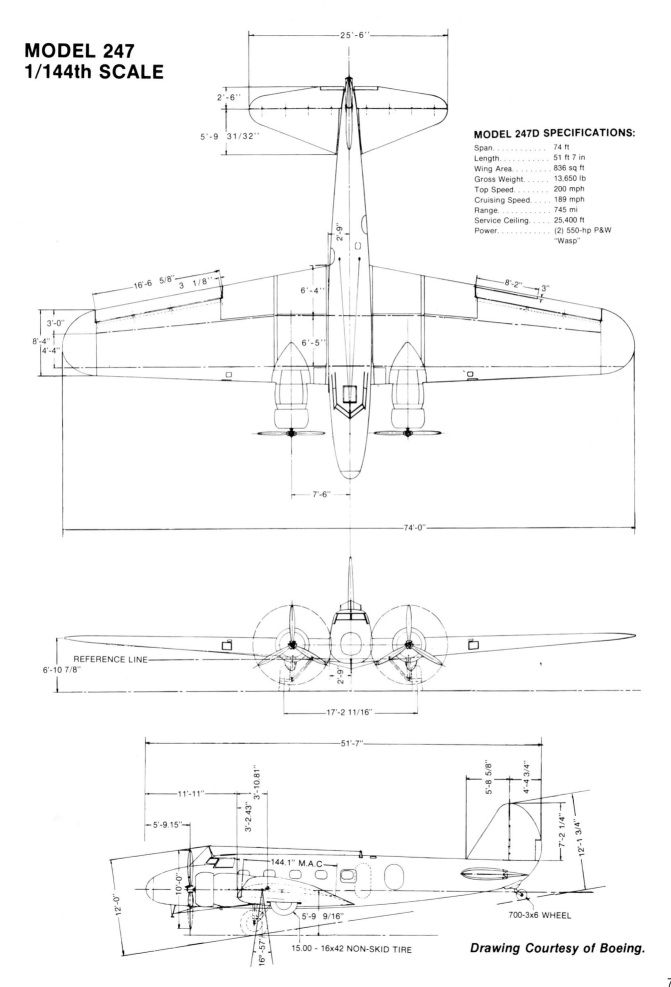

MODEL 247D SPECIFICATIONS:

Span . . . . 74 ft
Length . . . . 51 ft 7 in
Wing Area . . . . 836 sq ft
Gross Weight . . . . . . 13,650 lb
Top Speed . . . . 200 mph
Cruising Speed . . . . . 189 mph
Range . . . . 745 mi
Service Ceiling . . . . . 25,400 ft
Power . . . . (2) 550-hp P&W
                          "Wasp"

25'-6"
2'-6"
5'-9 31/32"
2'-9"
16'-6 5/8" 3 1/8"
6'-4"
8'-2" 3"
3'-0"
8'-4"
4'-4"
6'-5"
7'-6"
74'-0"

REFERENCE LINE
6'-10 7/8"
2'-9"
17'-2 11/16"

51'-7"
11'-11"
3'-10.81"
3'-2.43"
5'-9.15"
144.1" M.A.C.
10'-0"
12'-0"
16°-57'
15.00 - 16x42 NON-SKID TIRE
5'-9 9/16"
5'-8 5/8"
4'-4 3/4"
7'-2 1/4"
12'-1 3/4"
700-3x6 WHEEL

Drawing Courtesy of Boeing.

7

XB-15

The similarity between the XB-15 and the B-17 is apparent in this photograph. When it was built in 1937, the XB-15 was regarded as one of the wonders of the world.　*(Boeing 9430-B)*

The XB-15 was Boeing's Model 294, and was also designated XBLR-1, Project "A", and XC-105. The XB-15 designation was made in July, 1936. It was the first of the very heavy or "super" bombers, carrying a heavier load to a higher altitude than any aircraft in the world at the time it was built.

The first flight of the only XB-15 built was in October, 1937 with the famous Eddie Allen at the controls. On December 2, 1937 the aircraft was flown to Wright Field for testing by the Army Air Corps.

Among the innovations introduced by the new bomber was the first complete 110 V. A. C. electrical system with generators, not driven by the main engine, but by two auxiliary gasoline power plants within the plane. This "putt putt" or auxiliary power plant was adopted on the B-29. The wings of the XB-15 were built into the Pan American Airways CLIPPERS. Engines were accessible in flight, due to size of wing. Full radio equipment was installed, as was an automatic pilot, deicers, and wing flaps. This

was the first modern all-metal monoplane to have double-wheel retractable landing gear. It was the first long-range Army bomber outfitted with complete living and sleeping quarters for the crew. One of the many distinctly different features incorporated for the first time on an American aircraft was a flight engineer's station.

Some of the records made by this airplane were: (1) the carrying of a 31,167.6 pound payload to 8,200 feet on July 30, 1939, exceeding by 2,000 pounds the previous Russian record; (2) the carrying of a 4,409 pound payload 3,107 miles, at 166 miles per hour.

The design work on this aircraft started before the work on the B-17, and therefore it had an influence on the B-17 design. However the XB-15 did not fly until twenty-six months after the Model 299 prototype of the B-17. It then replaced the B-17 as the largest landplane in the United States.

It served as a transport in World War II under the XC-105 designation, and was dismantled in 1945 at a U.S. airbase in Central America.

XB-15 in flight.　*(Boeing 10520)*

Cockpit of the XB-15. Note the simplified instruments and the doors leading down to the nose section.　*(Boeing photo 10071-B)*

XB-15
1/288th SCALE

Wing span   --149 feet
Length: --87 feet, 7 inches
Wing area: --2,780 square feet
Gross weight: --70,706
Top speed: --200 mph
Cruising speed: --152 mph
Range: --5,130 miles
Service ceiling: --18,900 feet
Power: --Four 850 hp P&W Twin Wasp engines
Armament: --Six machine guns, 8,000 pounds of bombs

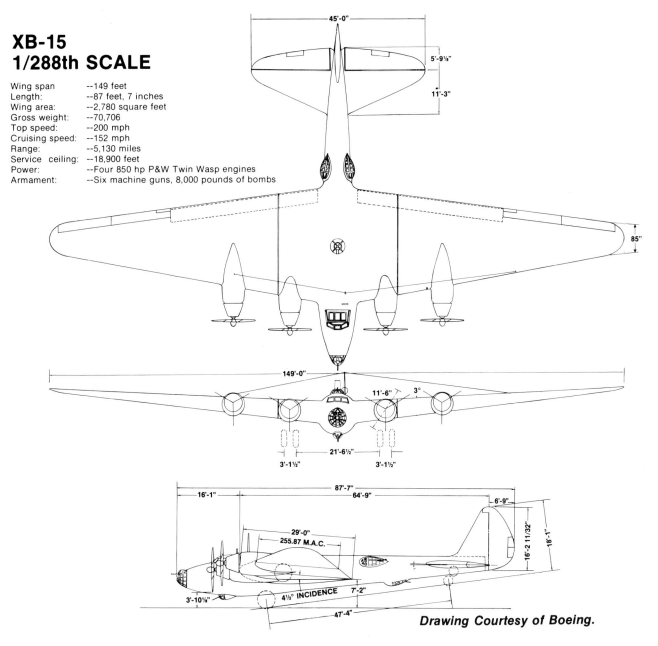

Drawing Courtesy of Boeing.

The XB-15. Note the dual wheel main landing gear.   **(Boeing 9428B)**

MODEL 299 THRU B-17B

The Y1B-17, also known as the YB-17, was the service test plane of the B-17 series, 13 of which were built. The model was virtually identical with the Model 299, but differed in having the new Wright Cyclone engines of 1,000 horsepower and single leg landing gear instead of the double strut type. (Boeing 11230-B)

Boeing's "Model Specification and History" on the Model 299 states, "Models 299, YB-17, Y1B-17A, and B-17B were designed and fabricated between the first conception and first production airplane." This would seem to indicate that Boeing considered these versions to be developmental aircraft, and the first production aircraft would then be the B-17C. For the purposes of this publication the versions up through the B-17B will also be considered as developmental aircraft and will be treated together.

MODEL 299

Although it crashed in an unfortunate accident as mentioned earlier, the Model 299 was quite successful, and the sound basic design of the prototype was carried throughout the B-17's production life. For example, the 103'9" wingspan, 19' wing root chord, and 1420 square feet of wing area was maintained on all variants.

Four single-row Pratt and Whitney SIEG (R-1690) Hornet engines, mustering 750 horsepower each, powered the prototype aircraft. A one-piece cowling surrounded each engine. The exhaust

stacks were located well aft on the top center line of the nacelles.

The Model 299 had a unique landing gear strut arrangement. The trunnion was located at the aft end of the wheel well and had a pair of main struts extending to either side of the wheel hub. These struts were supported by an "X" brace, and a multiple piece strut extended forward from the wheel hub. A double yoke and actuator formed the drag brace. One yoke straddled the wheel to attach at the hub. A second yoke mounted back-to-back with the lower yoke and mounted to the forward end of the wheel well. The two yokes hinged at their juncture and folded with gear retraction. A retracting screw actuator extended from the forward end of the wheel well and attached at the yoke hinge.

The tail wheel was supported by a forked strut which retracted forward into the fuselage leaving the wheel half exposed.

Five defensive single-mount machine gun positions were located in blisters on the top and bottom of the fuselage, on each side at the fuselage waist, and in the nose. Each gun was manually operated

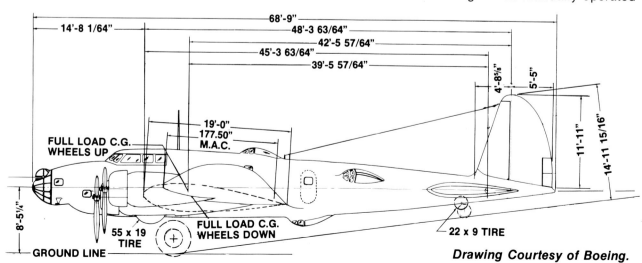

Drawing Courtesy of Boeing.

MODEL 299
1/144th SCALE

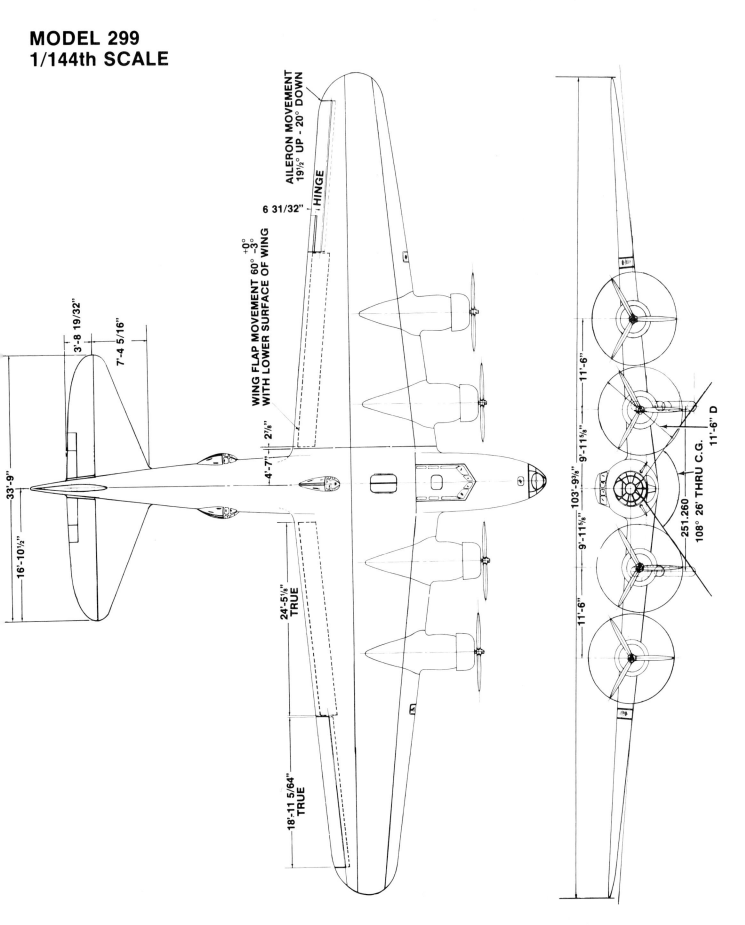

Drawing Courtesy of Boeing.

YB-17A taxis out for a flight.   *(G. S. Williams)*

and could be either .30 or .50 calibre.

Up to eight 600 pound bombs could be carried internally in the bomb bay, and the bomb bay arrangement was essentially the same throughout the B-17 production life. Outer bomb racks extended upward from the bomb bay door frame. The inner bomb racks formed a "V" and spanned the space between the top of the fuselage and a catwalk. Solenoids on the racks controlled the bomb releases, and pulleys at the top of the bomb bay were used to hoist the bombs into position. Doors on the forward and aft bulkheads of the bomb bay allowed access to the bay from either the forward cabin or waist station.

A crew of eight was carried on the Model 299 and consisted of a pilot, co-pilot, bombardier, navigator/radio operator, and four gunners.

After successful testing of the Model 299, the Army Air Corps placed an order for thirteen further aircraft initially designated Y1B-17.

Y1B-17

The YB-17 and Y1B-17 aircraft were one in the same. These 13 initial contract aircraft changed designation on November 20, 1936, prior to aircraft's first flight. The aircraft were identical to the prototype except for engines, landing gear, crew, and minor armament changes. The landing lights were faired into the wing leading edges instead of being protruding cylinders as on the prototype.

The P&W R-1690 Hornet engines were replaced with Wright R-1820-39 Cyclones; thereby increasing the available horsepower from 750 to 1,000 per engine.

Landing gear revisions included an aft retracting tail wheel and a completely redesigned main gear. The dual main strut of the prototype was replaced by a single oleo and a "V"-shaped drag strut. The wheel was mounted outboard of the main oleo. These changes were made in part to facilitate maintenance. With this design a jack could be placed directly under the oleo strut, the airplane could be jacked, and the wheel could be replaced without having to disassemble the axle.

YB-17A

Essentially the YB-17A (Y1B-17A) was a Y1B-17 built originally as a non-flying static test article. Successful testing with the Y1B-17 led to an Air Corps contract to convert the YB-17A into a flying aircraft. This aircraft was used as a test bed for the development of turbo-supercharged engine installations. Photographs of this aircraft reveal a variety of engine installations. Originally the supercharger turbines were mounted on top of the nacelles. The final location for the superchargers was on the bottom of the nacelles for the YB-17A and all subsequent production B-17s. The outboard engine installations were relatively straight forward with the engine exhaust manifolding into a single pipe running along the bottom of the nacelle to the turbine. On the inboard engines consideration had to be given to the wheel well and the manifold exited at the 4 and 8 o'clock positions on the number 2 and 3 engines, respectively. The manifold re-entered the nacelle aft of the main gear wheel to exit again along the lower centerline of the nacelle for connection with the turbine. Turbo-charged R-1820-51 engines were finally installed on the sole YB-17A. The performance with the turbo-supercharger brought about the purchase by the Army of 39 B-17Bs equipped with these turbo-superchargers.

B-17B

Larger flaps, enlarged rudder, and a revised nose comprised the externally visible changes on the B-17B. The belly bomb aiming window and greenhouse nose turret were replaced with a built-up plexiglas nose having a flat bomb aiming panel. This nose piece was retained through the B-17E. More side windows were added to the nose. The nose revision resulted in a 7-inch reduction in overall aircraft length. Additionally, the spinners were deleted from the propellers; to be carried later only on the XB-38.

Right side view of the right outboard nacelle on the Model 299. Note the landing light on the wing leading edge. On all versions after the Model 299 the landing lights were blended into the leading edge of the wing.   *(Boeing 8207)*

RETRACTING SCREW
3-6480
RETRACTING ASSY.
7-1021
YOKE-UPPER
9-1762
SUPPORT ASSY.
15-3671-1

YOKE-LOWER
9-1765

*Main landing gear as installed on the Model 299.
Note the two yokes and the retracting screw.
(Boeing 15-3435)*

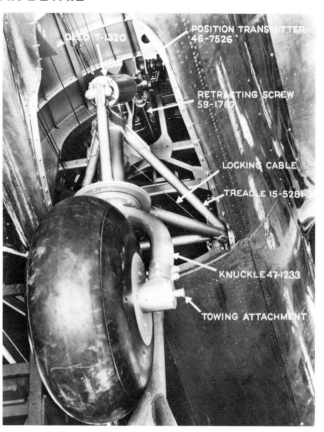

POSITION TRANSMITTER
46-7526
RETRACTING SCREW
59-1787
LOCKING CABLE
TREADLE 15-5281

KNUCKLE 47-1233

TOWING ATTACHMENT

*Tail wheel detail as installed on all versions of the
B-17 after the Model 299.   (Boeing 13740)*

*After the Model 299 all versions used the single strut
type of main landing gear. This installation is on a
B-17C. Note the smooth tire.   (Boeing 12770)*

*This photo shows the main landing gear on a B-17F.
Note the small changes from the B-17C at left. Also
note the treads on the tire.   (Boeing 26546)*

13

BOMB BAY DETAIL

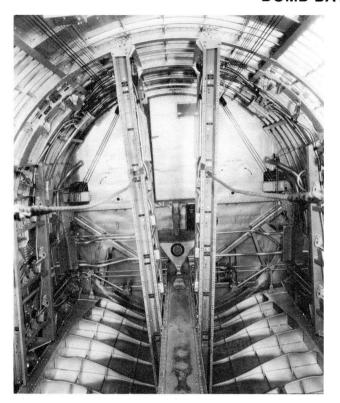

The bomb bay remained virtually the same throughout the entire B-17 series. Only a few changes to solenoids and bomb attach points were made. The photo on the left is looking forward (Boeing photo 8213) and the photo on the right is looking aft. **(Boeing 8212-B).**

In addition to bombs, the bomb bay could be fitted with long range fuel tanks as shown in these two photos. **(Boeing 13586)**

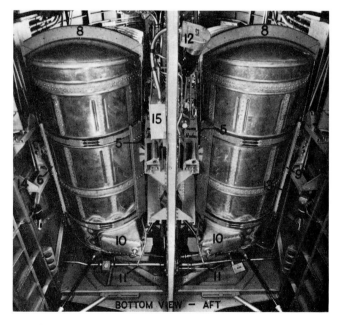

BOTTOM VIEW — AFT

1.	Cradle	10. Sump
2.	Tank	11. Vent
3.	Step Light	12. Bomb Door Retract. Motor
4.	Sight Gage	
5.	B-7 Bomb Shackle	13. Bomb Door Safety Switch
6.	Beam	
7.	Guard Rope	14. Bomb Door Position Transmitter
8.	Beam	
9.	Beam	15. Bomb Door Solenoid Shield

Outer bomb rack on left side.   *(Boeing 8192)*

Inner bomb rack looking up and forward.

(Boeing 8193)

NORDEN BOMBSIGHT

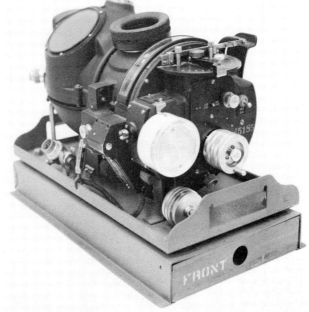

The Top Secret Norden Bombsight was one of the most closely guarded pieces of equipment in the B-17. It was considered to be the best bombsight in the world, and it made the B-17 and other U.S. bombers just that much more effective. Shown here are two close-up photos of a Norden Bombsight which was truly a marvelous piece of engineering in World War II.   *(J. Harlick)*

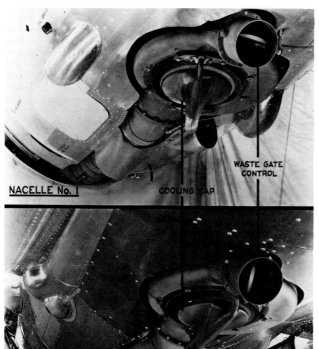

Top: The YB-17A was used to test supercharger installations for the B-17. In this photo the superchargers are mounted over the nacelles.

(G. S. Williams)

Middle: Here the YB-17A shows the supercharger installation closely approximating that use on later versions. (G. S. Williams)

Left: Supercharger detail as used on all versions after the YB-17A. Nacelle No. 3 was a mirror of No. 2, and No. 4 was a mirror of No. 1. (Boeing 13580)

Above: A factory fresh B-17B. Note the observation blister above the cockpit which is offset to the right. On the B-17C this blister was moved to the center-line. At the far left of the photo the landing light is visible, and it is flush with the wing leading edge. Compare this to the light on the Model 299 as shown on page 12. Also note the open crew entry door and the location of the windows on the nose.

(Boeing photo)

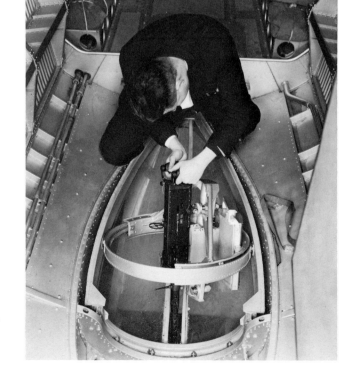

Right: Bottom gun mount as used up through the B-17B. The gun in the photo is aimed down and forward, and the awkward position of the gunner during firing could not have aided his marksmanship. *(Boeing 11076)*

Left and right side views show the details of the B-17B. A total of 39 B-17Bs was built. Photos taken on July 27, 1939 (Boeing 11754, 11750)

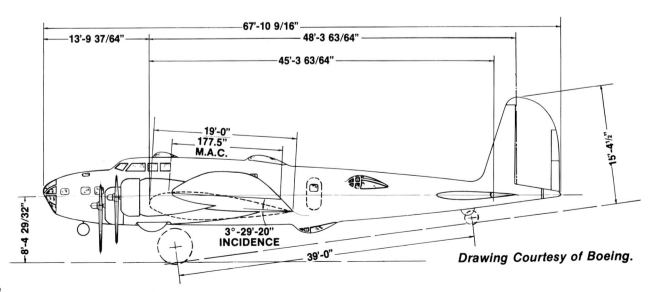

Drawing Courtesy of Boeing.

B-17B
1/144th SCALE

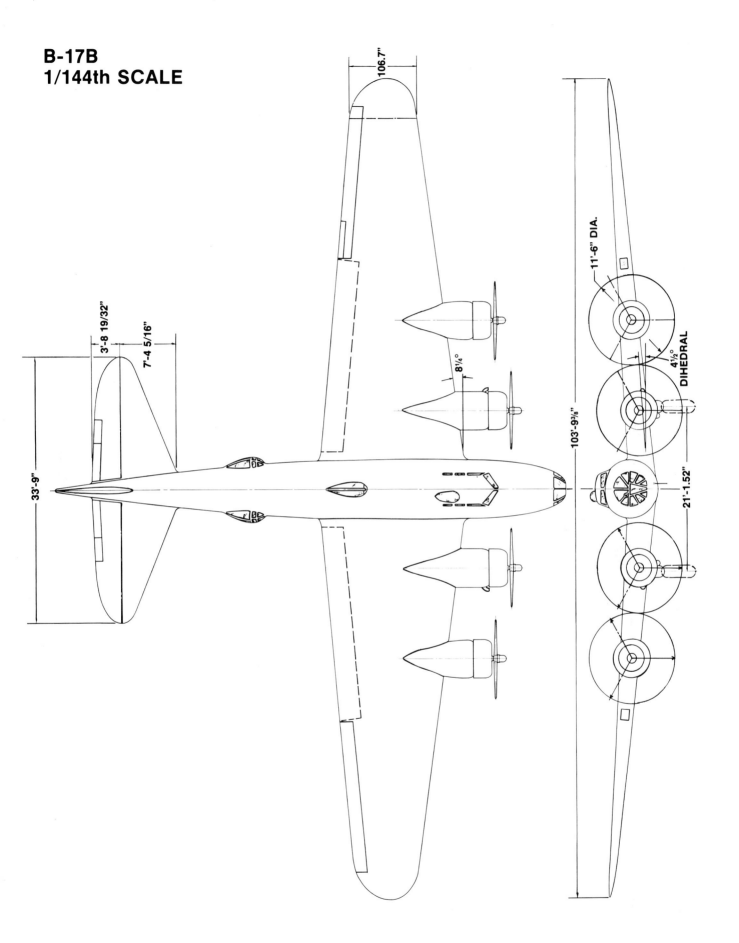

Drawing Courtesy of Boeing.

B-17C & B-17D

The B-17C (above) and B-17D (below) were almost identical in external appearance. Only the cowl flaps of the B-17D allowed the observer to tell the aircraft apart.   (Boeing 12879 and 15653)

A metal "bathtub" replaced the earlier belly blister on the B-17C. The plexiglas side blisters were replaced by flush gun ports. The single socket nose gun was deleted and a pair of .50 calibre guns were installed -- one in each side of the nose piece. Both the top and bottom gun positions had dual guns in lieu of the earlier single mounts. The top gun was a .50 calibre whereas the belly gun could be either .50 or .30 calibre with .30 being the preferred gun.

R-1820-65 Wright Cyclones replaced the earlier R-1820-51 engines, and the only visible external difference between the B-17C and the B-17D were the cowl flaps that were added to the B-17D.

The first twenty B-17Cs were assigned to England, and they began to arrive in country in the spring of 1941. They were designated "Fortress Is" by the British. The eighteen other B-17Cs were modified to B-17D standards and designated as B-17Ds.

In addition to the visible cowl flaps, the B-17D also incorporated leakproof fuel tanks and increased armament. B-17C and B-17D versions were the first B-17s to see combat in the Orient after Pearl Harbor.

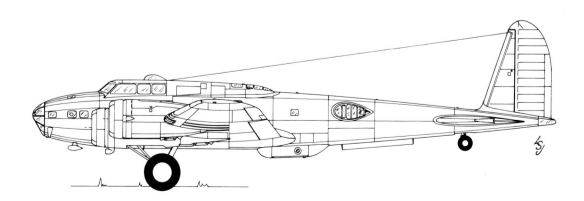

B-17C/D
1/144th SCALE

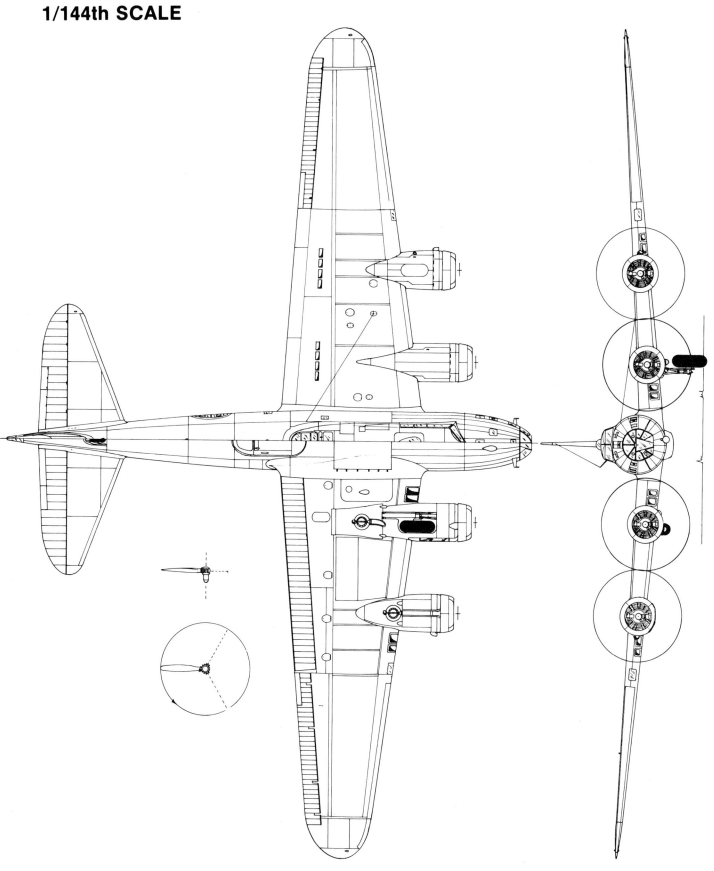

Right side engine nacelles on a B-17C. (Boeing 12838)

B-17C left inboard nacelle, engine, and propeller hub detail. (Boeing 12840)

Inboard side of the left outboard nacelle on a B-17C. (Boeing 12738)

B-17C left inboard engine firewall. (Boeing 12727)

B-17C left outboard engine firewall. (Boeing 12726)

Right nacelles and engines on a B-17C. Note the lack of cowl flaps.   *(Boeing P803)*

Right nacelles and engines on a B-17D showing the addition of cowl flaps.   *(Boeing P871)*

Looking aft in the left inboard nacelle wheel well of a B-17C.   *(Boeing 12786)*

Below, left and right: Number 3 power plant installation on a B-17C with the cowling removed.   *(Boeing 13725)*

1.	Exhaust Manifold	4.	Nose Cowl	7.	Starter Crank Support
2.	Starter Handle	5.	Panel	8.	Cowling (Not Shown)
3.	Engine Cowl Support	6.	Oil Cooler Scoop	9.	Ball Assembly

B-17C INTERIOR DETAIL

Cockpit looking forward. (Boeing 13731)

Cockpit looking aft. (Boeing 13731)

1.	Instrument Panel		13.	Parking Brake
2.	Starter Switches		14.	Life Raft Controls
3.	Fire Extinguisher Controls		15.	Fuel System Diagram
4.	Propeller Feathering		16.	Step Light Switch
5.	Warning Lights		17.	Data Card
6.	Oil Dilution Switches		18.	Commanders Dome
7.	Elevator Trim Tab Control		19.	Generator Switches
8.	Rudder Trim Tab Controls		20.	Command Receiver
9.	Attitude Control		21.	Cockpit Light
10.	Tail Wheel Lock		22.	Hand Fire Extinguisher
11.	Control Surface Lock		23.	Commanders Table
12.	Oxygen Bottles			

Cockpit, left side. (Boeing 13732)

Cockpit, right side. (Boeing 13732)

1.	Pilots Control Panel	12.	Propeller Control Lock	23.	Command Radio Junction
2.	Oxygen Regulator	13.	Automatic Flight Controls	24.	Spare Lamps
3.	Jack Box	14.	Booster Controls	25.	Land. Gear Warn. Horn
4.	Switch Box	15.	Booster & Mixture Lock	26.	Bombardiers Dome Light Switch
5.	Radio Filter	16.	Mixture Controls	27.	Ash Tray
6.	Engine Cross Feed	17.	Ignition Switches	28.	Thermocouple Selector
7.	Interphone	18.	Tank Selector Valves	29.	Oil Cooler Shutter
8.	Hand Fuel Pump	19.	Engine Selector Valves	30.	Hand Fuel Pump
9.	Throttles	20.	Cockpit Light	31.	Carb. Air Controls
10.	Throttle Lock	21.	Heat Damper Control	32.	Hydraulic Sys. Hand Pump
11.	Propeller Controls	22.	Microphone Amplifier	33.	Defroster Control Valve

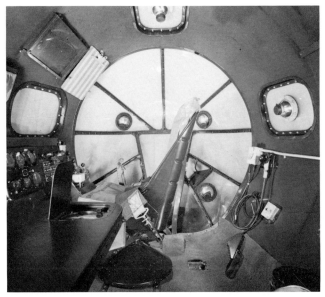

Nose compartment looking forward. Note the framing on the nose glass. **(Boeing 12852)**

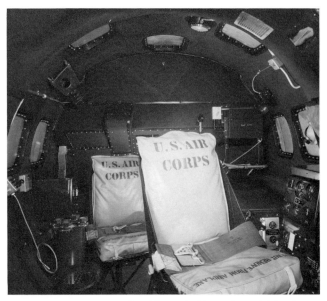

Nose compartment looking aft. Note the width of the seat belts. **(Boeing 12851)**

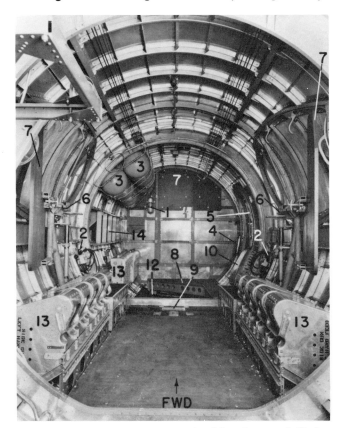

Rear gunner's compartment looking forward. Note the ammunition boxes for the waist guns.
(Boeing 14488)

Rear gunner's compartment looking aft. Note the location of the toilet. **(Boeing 14488)**

1. First Aid Kit	6. Gun Mount	11. Toilet
2. Interphone	7. Armor Plate	12. Gunner's Pit
3. Oxygen Bottles	8. Step	13. Ammunition Boxes
4. Hand Fire Extinguisher	9. Air Inlet	14. Entrance Ladder
5. Entrance Door	10. Gunner's Seat and Cushion	

B-17C ARMAMENT

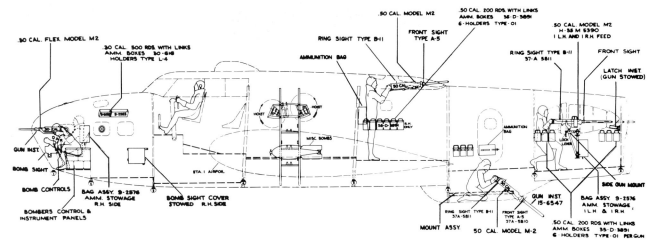

ARMAMENT, B-17C

Inside view of waist gun on a B-17C.

(Boeing)

Outside view of same gun mount.

(Both photos Boeing 12287)

Above: Outside top view of glass covering the radio compartment gun installation. (Boeing 12843)

Right: Inside view of twin gun mount installation in the radio room of a B-17C. (Boeing 15972)

This "bathtub" installation was used on the B-17C and B-17D replacing the belly gun blister used on earlier versions. (Boeing 12953)

B-17 s had two life rafts stowed in compartments on the upper fuselage sides just behind the cockpit. This photo shows the life raft stowed in the right side compartment on a B-17C. (Boeing 13734)

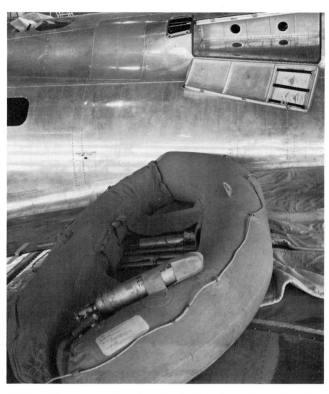

Life raft removed and partly inflated on the wing of a B-17C. (Boeing 12969)

Flap detail on a B-17C. (Boeing 12927)

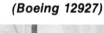

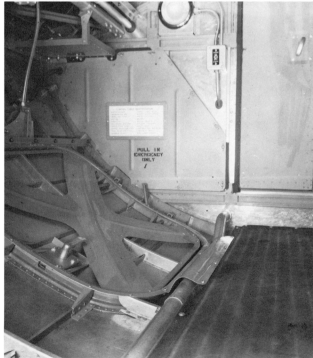

Interior view of the front entry hatch located just below the cockpit floor. (Boeing 12854)

Main entry door detail on a B-17C. This door is just behind the right wing root. (Boeing 12845)

B-17E

B-17Es. Note the shape of the nose glass and the periscopically aimed Sperry belly turret which replaced the "bathtub" as used on the B-17C and B-17D. The B-17E was also the first version to feature a top turret. Also note the open forward entry hatch on the aircraft in the foreground. This is the same hatch as shown at the bottom left of the previous page.
(Boeing 1031)

With the introduction of the B-17E came marked structural revisions to the aircraft. The entire empennage was redesigned, and the area of both the horizontal and vertical surfaces was increased. Top windows were added above the pilots on the B-17E and subsequent models. It was also seven tons heavier and 40 percent faster than the original Model 299.

A Sperry belly turret replaced the "bathtub". The turret was periscopically sighted from a blister located aft of the turret. At the 113th B-17E (41-2505), the Sperry ball turret was installed in lieu of the remote turret, and it was used on all of the subsequent B-17 models.

A twin .50 calibre Sperry upper turret was added just behind the pilots' compartment. Only the framed plexiglas dome and a small portion of the housing assembly protruded above the fuselage. Twin manual .50 calibre guns were added to the tail. The guns protruded through a canvas boot. A ring sight was mounted above the tail cone, aft of the gunner's greenhouse, and was moved by wires attached to the guns. Access to the compartment was gained from the tail wheel compartment through a small door in the bulkhead or through a side door. The latter access was generally reserved for emergency use. Single flexible .50 calibre guns were added to large windows in the waist position instead of the former tear-dropped shaped gun ports. Cheek guns appeared on some B-17s in the Pacific Theater as a result of field modifications.

In all, more than 400 changes were made in the B-17E, and by the time the contract was completed the Army placed a new contract for the B-17F which incorporated all of these changes.

B-17E in flight. Note the early remotely-sighted Sperry turret and the early national markings.(Boeing 2097)

"Esmeralda" (B-17E, 41-2600) undergoing maintenance in the field. Note the later Sperry belly turret and the B-17D in the background. (Boeing 1595)

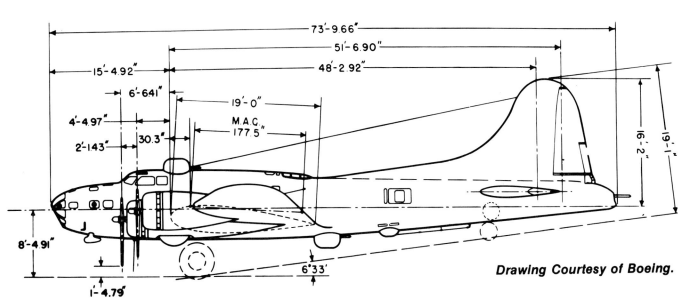

Drawing Courtesy of Boeing.

B-17E
1/144th SCALE

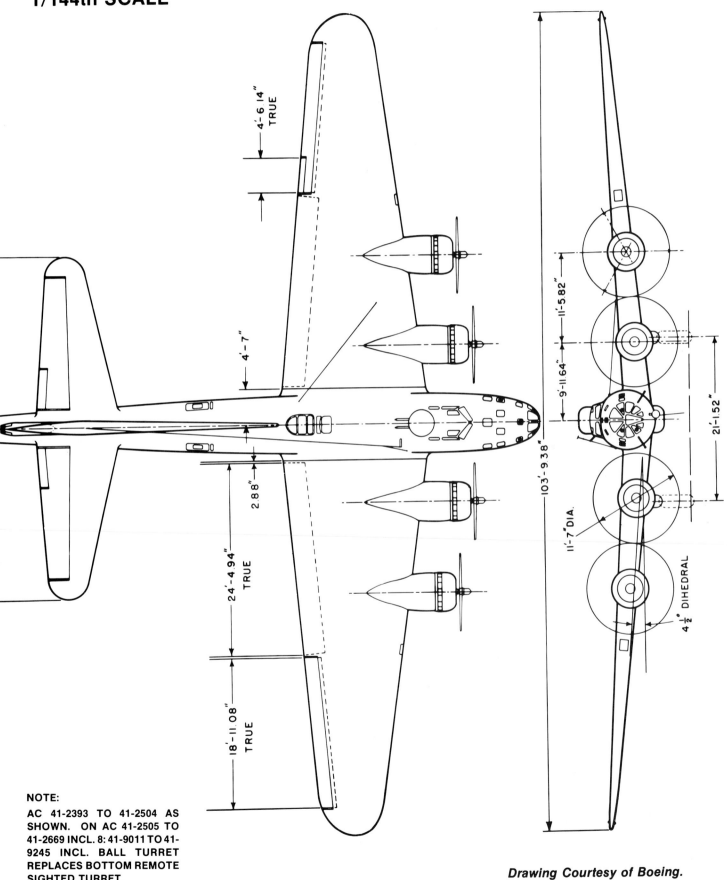

4'-6.14" TRUE

4'-7"

2.88"

24'-4.94" TRUE

18'-11.08" TRUE

103'-9.38"

11'-5.82"

9'-11.64"

21'-1.52"

11'-7" DIA.

4½° DIHEDRAL

NOTE:
AC 41-2393 TO 41-2504 AS SHOWN. ON AC 41-2505 TO 41-2669 INCL. 8: 41-9011 TO 41-9245 INCL. BALL TURRET REPLACES BOTTOM REMOTE SIGHTED TURRET.

Drawing Courtesy of Boeing.

Above: Remote belly turret looking aft (left) and looking forward (right). (Boeing 19784B/19785B)

Left: Exterior view of remotely sighted belly turret. (Boeing 18297B)

Below left: Uncrated ball turret reveals mounting ring and suspension structure. Hoops held oxygen bottles. Ammunition was carried internally. (Boeing P3846)

Below right: Rear view of Sperry turret with hatch open. (Boeing 4432)

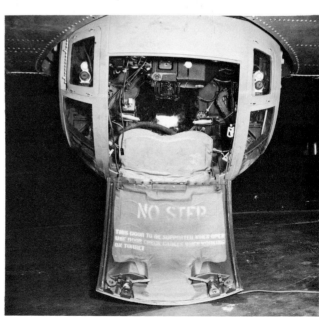

NOTE: B-17E details continued on page 41.

B-17 FLYING FORTRESS IN COLOR

Color photographs of the B-17 taken before and during World War II are very rare, and those that can be found usually show their age which is often over forty years. On the next eight pages are some of these rare photographs. While they may be old and not as perfect as photos taken today, they are obviously of more value and significance than new photographs taken of restored B-17's. Also included in this collection are cut-away drawings taken from a B-17 flight manual.

*Two views of a B-17B assigned to the **Materiel** Division at Wright Field. In the lower view note the crew boarding ladder and the unusual belly fairing.*   *(Smithsonian)*

B-17C of the 2nd Bomb Group. Note the commander's blister.   (Smithsonian)

Prototype B-17E.   (G.S. Williams via Boeing)

B-17F-85-BO, 42-30060, reveals its circa 1942 factory color scheme. Note the whip antenna under the navigator's compartment and the external bomb racks between the inboard engines and the fuselage.

(Boeing photo K14568)

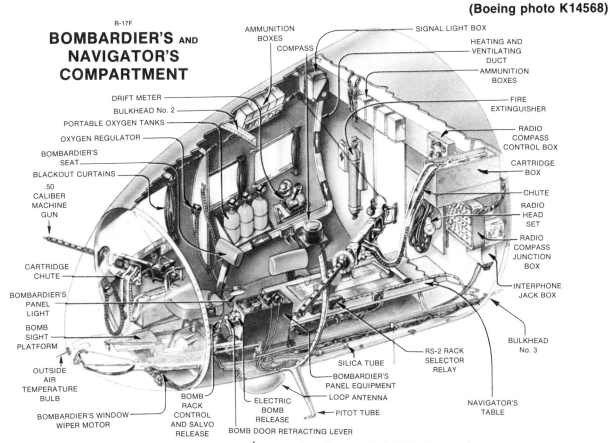

B-17F

BOMBARDIER'S AND NAVIGATOR'S COMPARTMENT

DRIFT METER
BULKHEAD No. 2
PORTABLE OXYGEN TANKS
OXYGEN REGULATOR
BOMBARDIER'S SEAT
BLACKOUT CURTAINS
.50 CALIBER MACHINE GUN
CARTRIDGE CHUTE
BOMBARDIER'S PANEL LIGHT
BOMB SIGHT PLATFORM
OUTSIDE AIR TEMPERATURE BULB
BOMBARDIER'S WINDOW WIPER MOTOR
BOMB RACK CONTROL AND SALVO RELEASE
ELECTRIC BOMB RELEASE
BOMB DOOR RETRACTING LEVER
SILICA TUBE
BOMBARDIER'S PANEL EQUIPMENT
LOOP ANTENNA
PITOT TUBE

AMMUNITION BOXES
COMPASS
SIGNAL LIGHT BOX
HEATING AND VENTILATING DUCT
AMMUNITION BOXES
FIRE EXTINGUISHER
RADIO COMPASS CONTROL BOX
CARTRIDGE BOX
CHUTE
RADIO HEAD SET
RADIO COMPASS JUNCTION BOX
INTERPHONE JACK BOX
BULKHEAD No. 3
RS-2 RACK SELECTOR RELAY
NAVIGATOR'S TABLE

This cut-away, and those on the next two pages were taken from a B-17F flight manual, and are courtesy of Boeing.

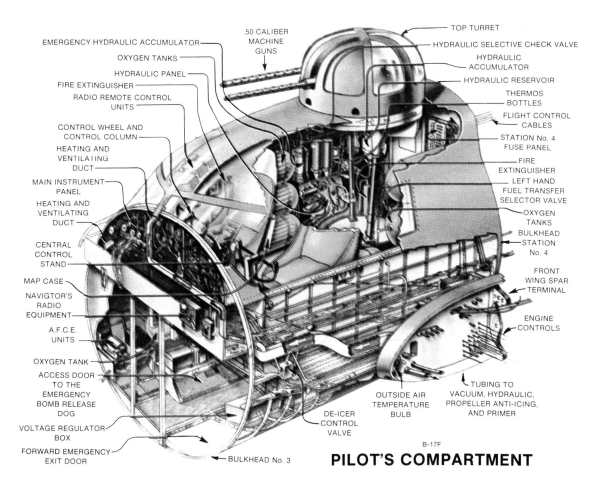

EMERGENCY HYDRAULIC ACCUMULATOR
OXYGEN TANKS
HYDRAULIC PANEL
FIRE EXTINGUISHER
RADIO REMOTE CONTROL UNITS
CONTROL WHEEL AND CONTROL COLUMN
HEATING AND VENTILATING DUCT
MAIN INSTRUMENT PANEL
HEATING AND VENTILATING DUCT
CENTRAL CONTROL STAND
MAP CASE
NAVIGTOR'S RADIO EQUIPMENT
A.F.C.E. UNITS
OXYGEN TANK
ACCESS DOOR TO THE EMERGENCY BOMB RELEASE DOG
VOLTAGE REGULATOR BOX
FORWARD EMERGENCY EXIT DOOR

.50 CALIBER MACHINE GUNS

TOP TURRET
HYDRAULIC SELECTIVE CHECK VALVE
HYDRAULIC ACCUMULATOR
HYDRAULIC RESERVOIR
THERMOS BOTTLES
FLIGHT CONTROL CABLES
STATION No. 4 FUSE PANEL
FIRE EXTINGUISHER
LEFT HAND FUEL TRANSFER SELECTOR VALVE
OXYGEN TANKS
BULKHEAD STATION No. 4
FRONT WING SPAR TERMINAL
ENGINE CONTROLS
TUBING TO VACUUM, HYDRAULIC, PROPELLER ANTI-ICING, AND PRIMER

OUTSIDE AIR TEMPERATURE BULB
DE-ICER CONTROL VALVE
BULKHEAD No. 3

B-17F
PILOT'S COMPARTMENT

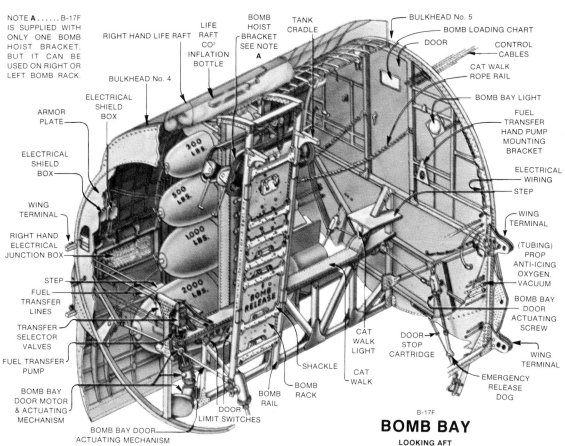

NOTE A......B-17F IS SUPPLIED WITH ONLY ONE BOMB HOIST BRACKET, BUT IT CAN BE USED ON RIGHT OR LEFT BOMB RACK.

RIGHT HAND LIFE RAFT
LIFE RAFT CO_2 INFLATION BOTTLE
BULKHEAD No. 4
ELECTRICAL SHIELD BOX
ARMOR PLATE
ELECTRICAL SHIELD BOX
WING TERMINAL
RIGHT HAND ELECTRICAL JUNCTION BOX
STEP
FUEL TRANSFER LINES
TRANSFER SELECTOR VALVES
FUEL TRANSFER PUMP
BOMB BAY DOOR MOTOR & ACTUATING MECHANISM
BOMB BAY DOOR ACTUATING MECHANISM

BOMB HOIST BRACKET SEE NOTE A
TANK CRADLE
BULKHEAD No. 5
BOMB LOADING CHART
DOOR
CONTROL CABLES
CAT WALK ROPE RAIL
BOMB BAY LIGHT
FUEL TRANSFER HAND PUMP MOUNTING BRACKET
ELECTRICAL WIRING
STEP
WING TERMINAL
(TUBING) PROP ANTI-ICING OXYGEN, VACUUM
BOMB BAY DOOR ACTUATING SCREW
WING TERMINAL
EMERGENCY RELEASE DOG
DOOR STOP CARTRIDGE
CAT WALK LIGHT
CAT WALK
SHACKLE
BOMB RACK
BOMB RAIL
DOOR LIMIT SWITCHES

300 LBS.
300 LBS.
1000 LBS.
BOMB RELEASE
2000 LBS.

B-17F
BOMB BAY
LOOKING AFT

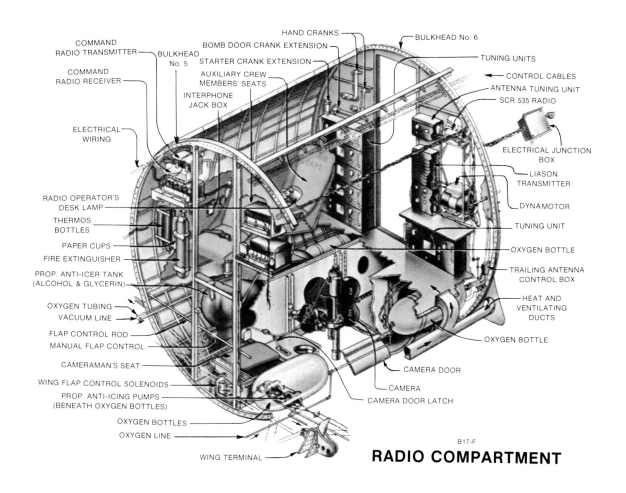

COMMAND RADIO TRANSMITTER
COMMAND RADIO RECEIVER
BULKHEAD No. 5
HAND CRANKS
BOMB DOOR CRANK EXTENSION
STARTER CRANK EXTENSION
AUXILIARY CREW MEMBERS' SEATS
INTERPHONE JACK BOX
BULKHEAD No. 6
TUNING UNITS
CONTROL CABLES
ANTENNA TUNING UNIT
SCR 535 RADIO
ELECTRICAL JUNCTION BOX
LIASON TRANSMITTER
DYNAMOTOR
TUNING UNIT
OXYGEN BOTTLE
TRAILING ANTENNA CONTROL BOX
HEAT AND VENTILATING DUCTS
OXYGEN BOTTLE
ELECTRICAL WIRING
RADIO OPERATOR'S DESK LAMP
THERMOS BOTTLES
PAPER CUPS
FIRE EXTINGUISHER
PROP. ANTI-ICER TANK (ALCOHOL & GLYCERIN)
OXYGEN TUBING
VACUUM LINE
FLAP CONTROL ROD
MANUAL FLAP CONTROL
CAMERAMAN'S SEAT
WING FLAP CONTROL SOLENOIDS
PROP. ANTI-ICING PUMPS (BENEATH OXYGEN BOTTLES)
OXYGEN BOTTLES
OXYGEN LINE
WING TERMINAL
CAMERA DOOR
CAMERA
CAMERA DOOR LATCH

B17-F

RADIO COMPARTMENT

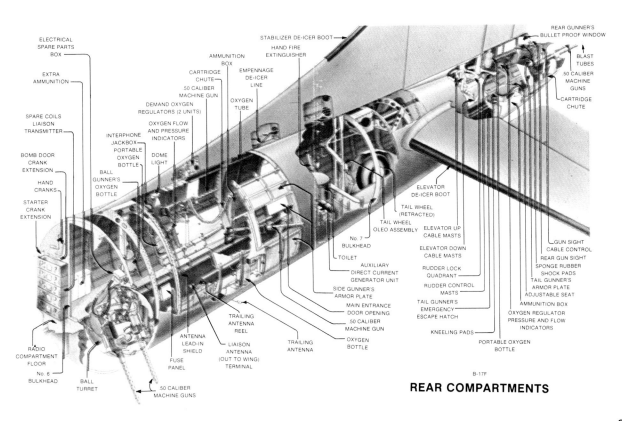

ELECTRICAL SPARE PARTS BOX
EXTRA AMMUNITION
SPARE COILS LIAISON TRANSMITTER
BOMB DOOR CRANK EXTENSION
HAND CRANKS
STARTER CRANK EXTENSION
RADIO COMPARTMENT FLOOR
No. 6 BULKHEAD
BALL TURRET
50 CALIBER MACHINE GUNS
FUSE PANEL
ANTENNA LEAD-IN SHIELD
LIAISON ANTENNA (OUT TO WING) TERMINAL
TRAILING ANTENNA REEL
BALL GUNNER'S OXYGEN BOTTLE
INTERPHONE JACKBOX PORTABLE OXYGEN BOTTLE
DOME LIGHT
OXYGEN FLOW AND PRESSURE INDICATORS
DEMAND OXYGEN REGULATORS (2 UNITS)
50 CALIBER MACHINE GUN
CARTRIDGE CHUTE
AMMUNITION BOX
OXYGEN TUBE
EMPENNAGE DE-ICER LINE
HAND FIRE EXTINGUISHER
STABILIZER DE-ICER BOOT
REAR GUNNER'S BULLET PROOF WINDOW
BLAST TUBES
50 CALIBER MACHINE GUNS
CARTRIDGE CHUTE
GUN SIGHT CABLE CONTROL
REAR GUN SIGHT
SPONGE RUBBER SHOCK PADS
TAIL GUNNER'S ARMOR PLATE
ADJUSTABLE SEAT
AMMUNITION BOX
OXYGEN REGULATOR PRESSURE AND FLOW INDICATORS
PORTABLE OXYGEN BOTTLE
KNEELING PADS
TAIL GUNNER'S EMERGENCY ESCAPE HATCH
RUDDER CONTROL MASTS
RUDDER LOCK QUADRANT
ELEVATOR DOWN CABLE MASTS
ELEVATOR UP CABLE MASTS
ELEVATOR DE-ICER BOOT
TAIL WHEEL (RETRACTED)
TAIL WHEEL OLEO ASSEMBLY
No. 7 BULKHEAD
TOILET
AUXILIARY DIRECT CURRENT GENERATOR UNIT
SIDE GUNNER'S ARMOR PLATE
MAIN ENTRANCE DOOR OPENING
50 CALIBER MACHINE GUN
OXYGEN BOTTLE
TRAILING ANTENNA

B-17F

REAR COMPARTMENTS

37

B-17E prototype in flight. Note early Sperry remote belly turret and sighting blister located just aft of the turret. Fabric control surfaces are painted OD. *(Boeing)*

B-17F-25-DL, 42-3259 "Snafu" of the 332nd BS, 94th BG, 8th AF, based at Bury St. Edmonds, Suffolk, England. *(USAF)*

B-17E, "Esmarelda," AF 41-2600 over western Washington. **(Boeing)**

View of the flight line at Patterson Field, Ohio during the war years. Note the different types of aircraft parked on the line. **(USAF)**

B-17F-60-BO, 42-29536, LL-A, "Mary Ruth, Memories of Mobile," of the 401st BS, 91st BG, 8th AF. (USAF)

B-17G-70-BO, 43-37635, VE-N, of the 532nd BS, 381st BG, 8th AF, based at Ridgewell, Essex, England.
(USAF)

Cockpit detail of a B-17E. Note the wooden control yokes and the throttle quadrant at center. The four smaller handles on the quadrant control propeller pitch. (Boeing 18288)

B-17E radio room looking forward. Note the control cables at the top on both sides. (Boeing 18195)

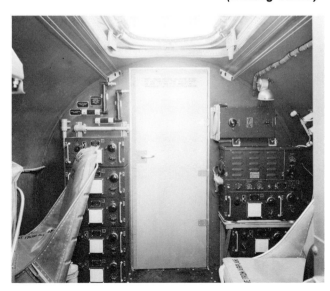

Radio room looking aft. The rear of the gun window is visible at the top center. (Boeing 21235)

Nose compartment looking forward from behind bombardier's seat.   *(Boeing 14494)*

Nose compartment looking aft. Note that the navigator's chair has a seat belt.   *(Boeing 14494)*

1. Armor Plate
2. Bombers Seat
3. Jack Box
4. Interphone
5. Pitot Heat Shield
6. Air Inlet
7. Gun Ball Mount
8. Navigators Table
9. Gun Stowage Bracket
10. Aperiodic Compass
11. Radio Compass Bearing Indicator
12. Navigation Instrument Case
13. Cockpit Light
14. Flight Instrument Access Door
15. Driftmeter Mount
16. Oxygen Bottles
17. Dome Light Switch
18. Ash Tray
19. Hot Air Inlet
20. Radio Compass Receiver

B-17F

Top: B-17F-50-VE. Compare the nose window arrangement on this aircraft with the windows on the aircraft in the middle photo.(Lockheed C3042)

Middle: B-17F-40-BO.   (Boeing 2505)

Right: Number 2 cowl installation (compare with B-17C on pages 22 and 23) on B-17F. Note the engine and exhaust manifold details. This double exposure shows the crew entry hatch in phantom.
(Boeing 23827)

B-17F- 95-BO, 230243, showing external bomb racks and flush cheek windows with guns. **(Boeing 3012)**

After the major design changes made in the B-17E, only small exterior variations appeared on the B-17F. A one-piece molded plexiglas nose was substituted for the earlier built-up nose glazing. Initially this was the only external difference between the B-17E and the B-17F. Paddle bladed propellers with the diameter increased by one inch to 11'7" were installed. This change necessitated a revision to the cowls to permit use of the larger chord propeller blades when feathered. These propellers were installed on the first B-17F-1-BO, serial number 41-24340.

Cheek guns were installed on some B-17Fs at modification centers prior to going to combat units. In production the cheek guns were installed starting with B-17F-55-BO (42-29467) and B-17F-15-DL (42-3004). The Lockheed Vega incorporation point for these guns is not known.

External bomb rack provisions were added with B-17F-30-BO (42-5050), B-17F-20-VE (42-5765), and B-17F-20-DL (42-3039). The rack positions were deleted with B-17F-95-BO (42-30232). Glide bomb attachments also appeared on B-17F-1-VE (42-5705) and B-17F-10-DL (42-2929). With B-17F-75-DL (42-3504) the first factory installed Bendix chin turrets appeared. These were to become standard on the B-17G. Lastly, an astrodome was added on the nose of the B-17F beginning with B-17F-45-BO, B-17F-15-DL, and B-17F-15-VE.

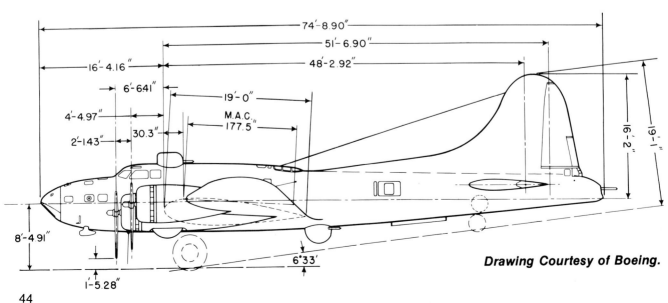

Drawing Courtesy of Boeing.

B-17F
1/144th SCALE

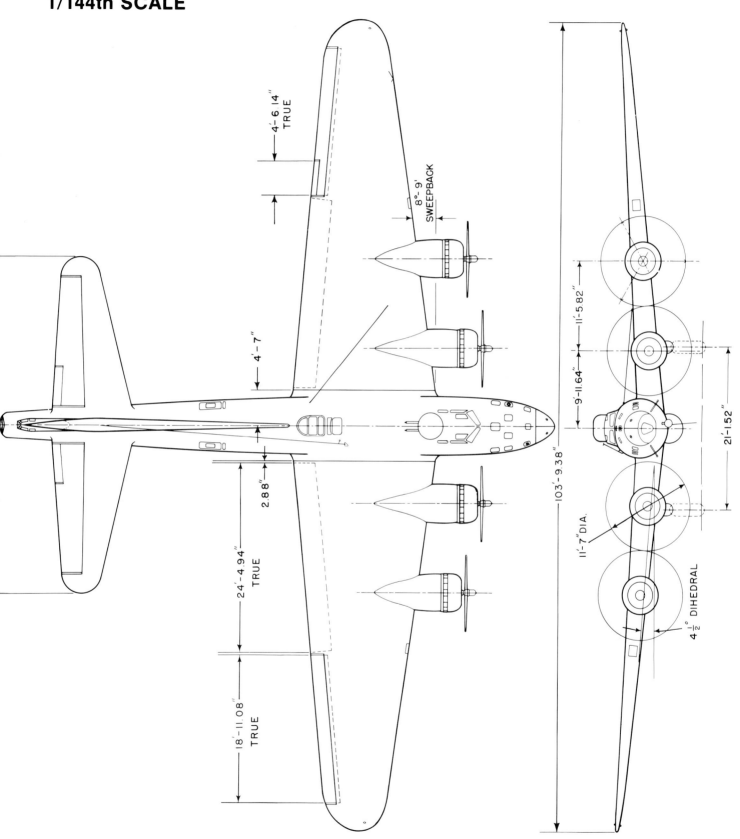

4'-6.14" TRUE

8°-9' SWEEPBACK

4'-7'

2.88" TRUE

24'-4.94" TRUE

18'-11.08" TRUE

103'-9.38"

11'-5.82"

9'-11.64"

21'-1.52

11'-7" DIA.

4½° DIHEDRAL

Drawing Courtesy of Boeing.

45

B-17F INTERIOR DETAIL

B-17F main instrument panel.　　　　　　　　　　　　　　　　　**(Boeing 38509)**

1. Fluorescent lights
2. Voltmeter
3. Radio Compass
4. Hydraulic Pressure Warning Light
5. Light On--bomb bay doors open
6. Bomb Release
7. Vacuum Warning Light
8. P.D. 1 Equipment
9. Altimeter
10. Visual Indicator Blind Landing Cutout
11. Marker Beacon
12. Air Speed Indicator
13. Gyro Compass
14. Turn & Bank Indicator
15. Flight Indicator
16. Manifold Pressure Indicator
17. Tachometer
18. Fuel Pressure Indicator
19. Oil Pressure
20. Free Air Temperature Indicator
21. Fuel Tank Gauge
22. Carburetor Air Temperature
23. Oil Temperature
24. Cylinder Head Temperature
25. Flap Position Indicator
26. Tail Wheel Lock
27. Landing Gear Down
28. Bomber Call Button
29. Rate of Climb Indicator
30. Propeller Feathering Buttons
31. Airspeed Tube Static Pressure
32. Oxygen Cylinder Pressure Indicators
33. Vacuum Gage
34. Supply Warning Light
35. Oxygen Flow Indicators
36. Oil Pressure--Main System
37. Oil Pressure--Emergency System

Exterior of cockpit and nose of B-17F showing cheek windows and astrodome.　**(Boeing 3282)**

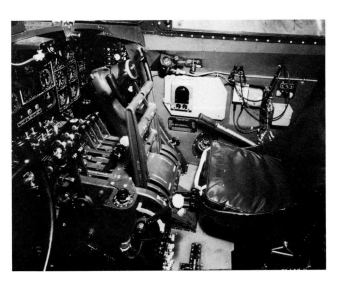

Right side of B-17F cockpit. Note that wood was no longer used on the control yokes. **(Boeing 25348)**

46

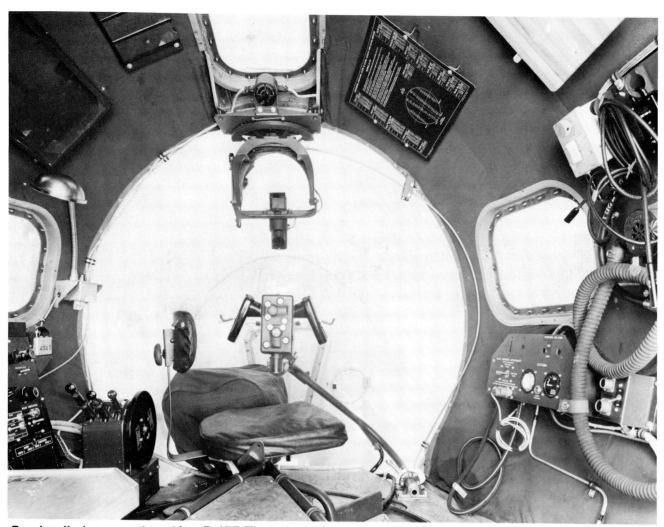

Bombardier's compartment in a B-17F. The yoke at the center is for controlling the chin turret which appeared on late B-17F s, and became standard on the B-17G. The yoke could be moved to the right when bombing became the primary task of the bombardier. (Boeing 37897)

Bombardier's panel and release stand on left side. (Boeing 37891)

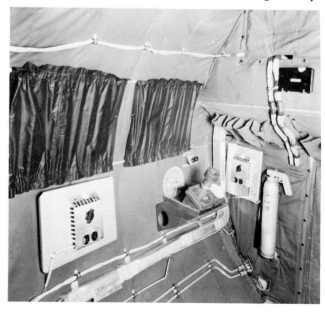

Bombardier's compartment, right side, looking aft. Note the curtains. (Boeing 37896)

B-17F ARMAMENT

After suffering devastating frontal attacks, the need for improved firepower was recognized. At modification centers, where other operational equipment was being installed, a new forward gun mount was added to later aircraft. Four tubular frames attached to the forward-most fuselage frame supported a box structure mounted in the apex of the nose glazing. This box structure served as the pivot mount for either single or dual .50 calibre machine guns. A cable and spring device was attached to the gun cradle near the gun breach to relieve the gun weight for the gunner.

(Left: Seely, Right: Fawkes)

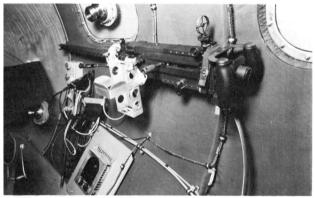

Internal stowage provisions for .50 calibre nose or cheek gun. **(Boeing 25244B)**

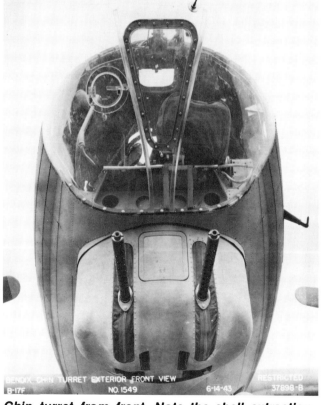

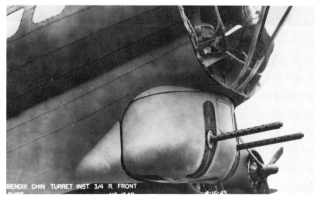

Bendix chin turret as installed on a B-17F. Note the zipped canvas gun slot covers. **(Boeing 37899)**

Chin turret from front. Note the shell extraction slots. This turret became standard on B-17Gs. **(Boeing 37898)**

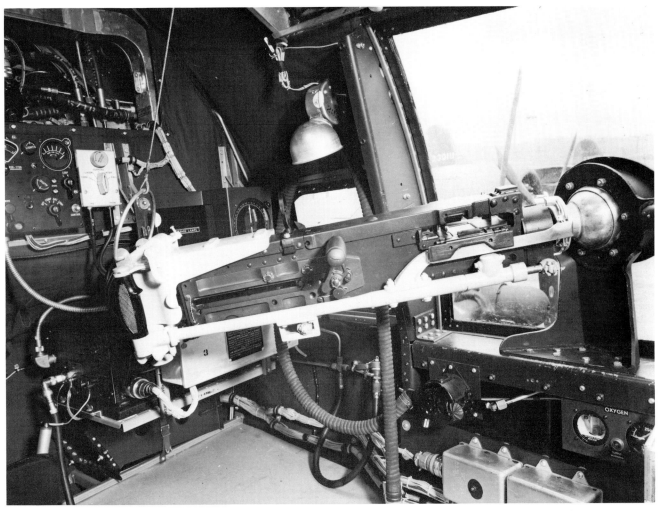

Interior view of left cheek gun on a B-17F. Note that the window was mounted flush with the fuselage side.
(Boeing 34711)

The top turret on the B-17E was used on the B-17F and later on the B-17G with a higher dome.(Boeing)

Close-up of a top turret on a B-17F.(Boeing 3647)

Top Left: Radio compartment gun in firing position. This gun is mounted on a ring mount, and the window area is opened for firing. Note the wooden ammunition box and the flexible ammunition feed belt. **(Boeing 33012)**

Top Right: Radio room on B-17F looking aft with gun in stowed position. Compare this photo with the one on page 27 showing the twin mount on a B-17C. **(Boeing 33218)**

Left: In August 1944 the ring mount for this gun was replaced with the installation shown here. It was subsequently discontinued altogether on late model B-17Gs. **(Boeing 5076)**

Interior view of waist gun positions. This view shows to good effect why these positions were staggered on late model B-17Gs to keep the gunners from bumping into each other in the heat of battle. (Boeing 1624)

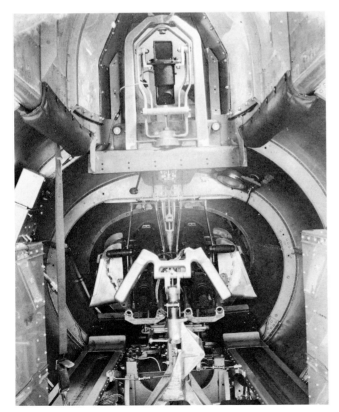

Interior view of tail gun installation on a B-17F.
(Boeing 19752)

Tail gun position from directly behind. Note gunner's head and sight. (Boeing photo)

A B-17F-35-DL in flight. This photo clearly shows the added cheek guns in their enlarged windows, the astro-dome with a small window on either side, and the Sperry top turret. (Douglas C16318)

External bomb racks were carried on a number of B-17Fs. See page 44 for block number breakdown. (Boeing HS-523)

Flying shot of a B-17F showing underside detail. Note the intakes and light on the leading edge of the wing. Also note the whip antenna under the nose, the Sperry turret, and the clear nosepiece which deleted the metal framework found on earlier models. As an early -F model, this aircraft does not have the astrodome or the larger cheek windows for the gun mounts.   *(Boeing 2480)*

A later B-17F than the one above this aircraft, a B-17F-55-BO, shows the added cheek guns and astrodome. Also carefully note the small window to the side of the astrodome. A similar window straddled the astrodome on the right side.   *(Boeing 31693)*

B-17G

An early B-17G. Note that the top turret has a higher dome than the turrets used on the B-17E and B-17F. Note also that there are no cheek guns on this aircraft as these were not installed until the B-17G-60-BO, B-17G-25-DL, and B-17G-35-VE production blocks. *(G. S. Williams)*

The camouflaged B-17G-30-DL is the last of the Douglas-built-30 production block, while the natural metal aircraft is the first of the B-17G-35-DL production block. *(Douglas C16318)*

This Lockheed-Vega B-17G-40-VE has OD anti-glare panels in front of the cockpit and on the inboard sides of the engine nacelles and cowlings. The waist gun window is covered with protective material. **(Lockheed 5310)**

The B-17G was a continuation of the B-17F contract, and many more changes appeared. The B-17G revealed numerous armament changes. All B-17Gs were manufactured with the Bendix chin turret. Cheek mounts with .50 calibre machine guns, originally on the B-17Fs, reappeared with B-17G-60-BO (42-102944), B-17G-35-VE (42-97836), and B-17G-25-DL (42-37989). The staggered waist gun positions came late in the program with B-17G-50-BO (42-102379), B-17G-50-VE (44-8101), and B-17G-25-DL (42-37989). Enclosed waist gun positions appeared in production with B-17G-50-BO (42-102379) and B-17G-25-DL (42-37989).

The radio compartment gun position was enclosed with B-17G-85-BO (43-38474), B-17G-65-VE (44-8401), and B-17G-45-DL (44-6251). This gun position was eliminated from production with B-17G-105-BO) (43-39206), B-17G-85-VE (44-8817), and B-17G-75-DL (44-83236). The top turret had a higher framed plexiglas dome giving the gunner more headroom and visibility.

Though numerous B-17s were retrofitted with Cheyenne tail turrets at the United Air Lines Modification Center at Cheyenne, Wyoming, many kits were installed at field modification centers in England. The first production Cheyenne turrets appeared with B-17G-80-BO (43-38473), B-17G-55-VE (44-8287), and B-17G-25-DL (42-37989). This modification resulted in a five inch decrease in overall aircraft length.

As a final change, the right hand pitot probe horn was deleted with the advent of the B-17G. In 1946 a B-17G set the world's altitude record for a four-engine airplane of 43,499 feet.

This ad appeared in a Boeing publication offering a B-17G at a reduced price to Boeing's women employees. It was one of many efforts made during the war to sell bonds to fund America's war effort. While it is on the humorous side, it was a most serious business. What is most interesting about the ad is the cost of a B-17G. Compare it to today's cost of a B-1 or even a B-52! **(Ad courtesy of Boeing)**

B-17G
1/144th SCALE

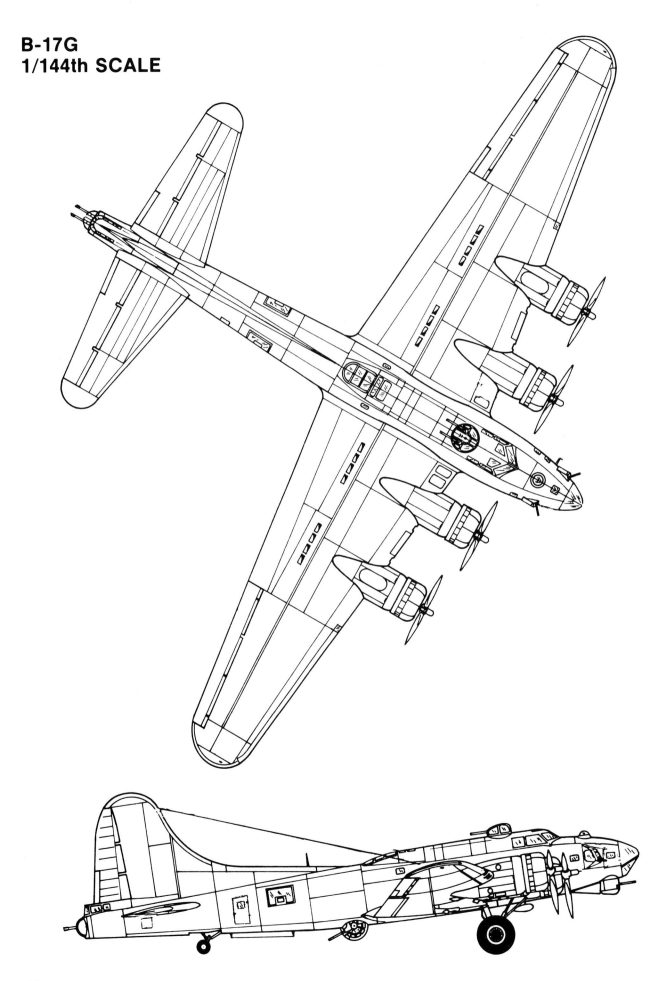

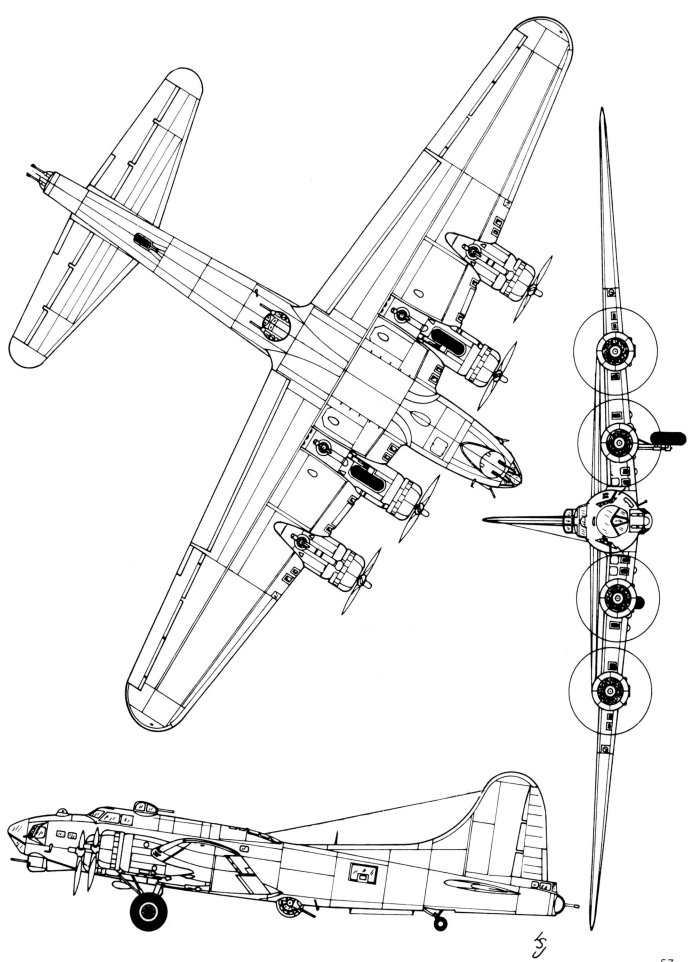

The last B-17G-5-BO off the production line is shown here with its top turret glazing and chin gun fairing removed.
(P. M. Bowers)

Seven camouflaged B-17Gs on the Douglas assembly line at Long Beach. Painting sub-assemblies prior to final assembly is a trait carried through by Douglas today. *(McDonnell-Douglas C14867)*

B-17Gs ON THE ASSEMBLY LINE

These photos of B-17Gs on the assembly lines at Boeing show many steps in the construction of the B-17, and many of the details of the aircraft.
(Boeing photos)

B-17G INTERIOR DETAIL

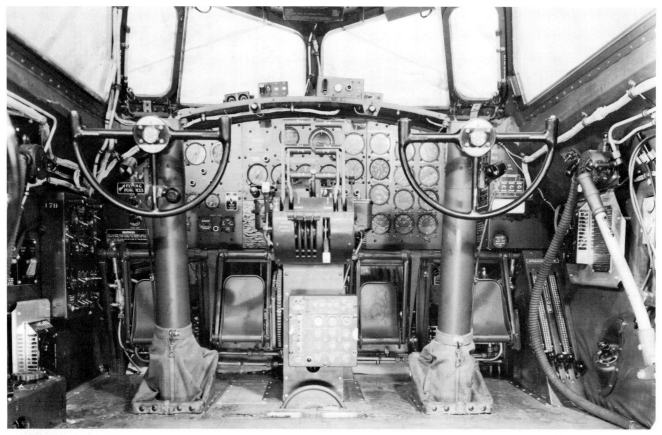

Cockpit in a B-17G.   *(Boeing 46668)*

Center console and automatic flight control equipment.   *(Boeing 46666)*

Cockpit ceiling controls.   (Boeing 46667)

View looking aft through the bomb bay and radio compartment on a B-17G.   (J. W. Bethards)

Pilot's side panel (left side).   (Boeing 46670)

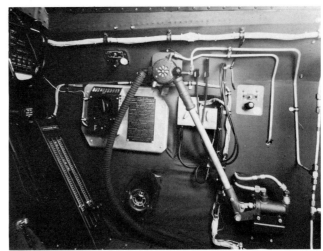

Co-pilot's side panel (right side).   (Boeing 46669)

Front view of a B-17G showing chin turret, cheek guns, and bombardier's aiming panel to good effect. (Boeing 4702)

Late B-17G showing cheek gun and chin turret. Note the lack of metal framing on the blown nose glass. (Boeing 4722)

K-6 gun mount in the left hand waist position on a B-17G-105-BO. This mount was first installed on B-17G-50-BO, B-17G-50-VE, and B-17G-40-DL block aircraft. Note the armor plate below the window and the reflector sight on the gun. (Boeing 36835)

Note the flatness of the Cheyenne tail turret. Ride-smothing spoilers were added in September 1944. (Boeing 82177B)

A B-17G-45-BO in flight. Note the absence of cheek guns which did not appear until the B-17G-60-BO production block. (Boeing 4365)

A B-17G-80-BO running up at Boeing Field. Note the crew entry door just aft of the national insignia. Cheek guns are installed on this aircraft, but the serial is 365 numbers earlier than the first B-17G-80-BO to receive the Cheyenne turret. (Boeing 4981)

B-17 PRODUCTION BLOCKS & SERIALS

TYPE	SERIAL	TYPE	SERIAL	TYPE	SERIAL	TYPE	SERIAL
Y1B-17	36-149/36-161	B-17F-75-DL	42-3504/42-3562	B-17G-1-BO	42-31032/42-31131	B-17G-80-BO	43-38074/43-38273
Y1B-17A	37-369	B-17G-5-DL	42-3563	B-17G-5-BO	42-31132/42-31231	B-17G-85-BO	43-38274/43-38473
B-17B	38-211/38-220	B-17F-30-BO	42-5050/42-5078	B-17G-10-BO	42-31232/42-31331	B-17G-90-BO	43-38474/43-38673
B-17B	38-221/38-223	B-17F-35-BO	42-5079/42-5149	B-17G-15-BO	42-31332/42-31431	B-17G-95-BO	43-38674/43-38873
B-17B	38-258/38-270	B-17F-40-BO	42-5150/42-5249	B-17G-20-BO	42-31432/42-31631	B-17G-100-BO	43-38874/43-39073
B-17B	38-583/38-584	B-17F-45-BO	42-5250/42-5349	B-17G-25-BO	42-31632/42-31731	B-17G-105-BO	43-39074/43-39273
B-17B	38-610	B-17F-50-BO	42-5350/42-5484	B-17G-30-BO	42-31732/42-31931	B-17G-110-BO	43-39274/43-39508
B-17B	39-1/39-10	B-17F-1-VE	42-5705/42-5709	B-17G-35-BO	42-31932/42-32116	B-17G-40-DL	44-6001/44-6125
B-17C	40-2042/40-2079	B-17F-5-VE	42-5710/42-5724	B-17G-80-DL	42-37714/42-37715	B-17G-45-DL	44-6126/44-6250
B-17D	40-3059/40-3100	B-17F-10-VE	42-5725/42-5744	B-17G-10-DL	42-37716	B-17G-50-DL	44-6251/44-6500
B-17E	41-2393/41-2669	B-17F-15VE	42-5745/42-5764	B-17F-80-DL	42-37717/42-37720	B-17G-55-DL	44-6501/44-6625
B-17E	41-9011/41-9245	B-17F-20-VE	42-5765/42-5804	B-17G-10-DL	42-37721/42-37803	B-17G-60-DL	44-6626/44-6750
B-17F-1-BO	41-24340/41-24389	B-17F-25-VE	42-5805/42-5854	B-17G-15-DL	42-37804/42-37893	B-17G-65-DL	44-6751/44-6875
B-17F-5-BO	41-24390/41-24439	B-17F-30-VE	42-5855/42-5904	B-17G-20-DL	42-37894/42-37988	B-17G-70-DL	44-6876/44-7000
B-17F-10-BO	41-24440/41-24439	B-17F-35-VE	42-5905/42-5954	B-17G-25-DL	42-37989/42-38083	B-17G-45-VE	44-8001/44-8100
B-17F-15-BO	41-24490/41-24503	B-17F-40-VE	42-5955/42-6029	B-17G-30-DL	42-38084/42-38213	B-17G-50-VE	44-8101/44-8200
B-17F-20-BO	41-24504/41-24539	B-17F-45-VE	42-6030/42-6104	B-17G-1-VE	42-39758/42-39857	B-17G-55-VE	44-8201/44-8300
B-17F-25-BO	41-24540/41-24584	B-17F-50-VE	42-6105/42-6204	B-17G-5-VE	42-39858/42-39957	B-17G-60-VE	44-8301/44-8400
B-17F-27-BO	41-24585/41-24639	B-17F-55-BO	42-29467/42-29531	B-17G-10-VE	42-39958/42-40057	B-17G-65-VE	44-8401/44-8500
B-17F-1-DL	42-2964/42-2966	B-17F-60-BO	42-29532/42-29631	B-17G-40-BO	42-97058/42-97172	B-17G-70-VE	44-8501/44-8600
B-17F-5-DL	42-2967/42-2978	B-17F-65-BO	42-29632/42-29731	B-17G-45-BO	42-97173/42-97407	B-17G-75-VE	44-8601/44-8700
B-17F-10-DL	42-2979/42-3003	B-17F-70-BO	42-29732/42-29831	B-17G-15-VE	42-97436/42-97535	B-17G-80-VE	44-8701/44-8800
B-17F-15-DL	42-3004/42-3038	B-17F-75-BO	42-29832/42-29931	B-17G-20-VE	42-97536/42-97635	B-17G-85-VE	44-8801/44-8900
B-17F-20-DL	42-3039/42-3073	B-17F-80-BO	42-29932/42-30031	B-17G-25-VE	42-97636/42-97735	B-17G-90-VE	44-8901/44-9000
B-17F-25-DL	42-3074/42-3148	B-17F-85-BO	42-30032/42-30131	B-17G-30-VE	42-97736/42-97835	B-17G-75-DL	44-83236/44-83360
B-17F-30-DL	42-3149/42-3188	B-17F-90-BO	42-30132/42-30231	B-17G-35-VE	42-97836/42-97935	B-17G-80-DL	44-83361/44-83485
B-17F-35-DL	42-3189/42-3228	B-17F-95-BO	42-30232/42-30331	B-17G-40-VE	42-97936/42-98035	B-17G-85-DL	44-83486/44-83585
B-17F-40-DL	42-3229/42-3283	B-17F-100-BO	42-30332/42-30431	B-17G-50-BO	42-102379/42-102543	B-17G-90-DL	44-83586/44-83685
B-17F-45-DL	42-3284/42-3338	B-17F-105-BO	42-30432/42-30531	B-17G-55-BO	42-102544/42-102743	B-17G-95-DL	44-83686/44-83863
B-17F-50-DL	42-3339/42-3393	B-17F-110-BO	42-30532/42-30616	B-17G-60-BO	42-102744/42-102978	B-17G-95-DL	44-83864/44-83885
B-17F-55-DL	42-3394/42-3422	B-17F-115-BO	42-30617/42-30731	B-17G-35-DL	42-106984/42-107233	B-17G-95-VE	44-85492/44-85591
B-17F-60-DL	42-3423/42-3448	B-17F-120-BO	42-30732/42-30831	B-17G-65-BO	43-37509/43-37673	B-17G-100-VE	44-85592/44-85691
B-17F-65-DL	42-3449/42-3482	B-17F-125-BO	42-30832/42-30931	B-17G-70-BO	43-37674/43-37873	B-17G-105-VE	44-85692/44-85791
B-17F-70-DL	42-3483/42-3503	B-17F-130-BO	42-30932/42-31031	B-17G-75-BO	43-37874/43-38073	B-17G-110-VE	44-85792/44-85841

DIMENSIONS

(Actual)

DIMENSIONS	AIRCRAFT						
	Model 299 ("XB-17")	Y1B-17 (YB-17) YB-17A	B-17B	B-17C B-17D	B-17E	B-17F	B-17G
Wing Span (ft. in.)	103 9.36	103 9.36	103 9.36	103 9.36	103 9.36	103 9.36	103 9.36
Wing Root Chord (ft.)	19	19	19	19	19	19	19
Wing Area (sq. ft.)	1420	1420	1420	1420	1420	1420	1420
Aileron Span (ft. in.)	18 11.00	18 11.25	18 11.25	18 11.25	18 11.08	18 11.08	18 11.08
Flap Span(ft. in.)	24 5.12	24 5.12	24 5.12	24 5.12	24 4.94	24 4.94	24 4.94
Length (ft. in.)	68 9.00	68 9.00	67 10.20	67 10.20	73 9.66	74 8.90	74 8.90 74 3.90*
Height (ft. in.)	14 11.94	14 11.94	14 11.94	15 4.50	19 1.00	19 1.00	19 1.00
Horizontal Stabilizer Span (ft. in.)	33 9.00	33 9.00	33 9.00	33 9.00	43 0.00	43 0.00	43 0.00
Horizontal Stabilizer Root Chord (ft. in.)	11 0.90	11 0.78	11 0.78	11 0.78	11 2.40	11 2.40	11 2.40
Vertical Tail Area (sq. ft.)	82.2	82.2	89.3	89.3	180.07	180.7	180.7
Horizontal Tail Area (sq. ft.)	254.4	254.4	245.4	331.1	331.1	331.1	331.1
MLG Track (ft. in)	20 11.25	20 11.25	21 1.52	21 1.52	21 1.52	21 1.52	21 1.52
MLG Dia. (in.)	55.00	55.00	55.00	55.00	55.00	55.00	56.00
Tail Wheel Dia. (in.)	22.00	22.00	23.00	23.00	26.00	26.00	26.00
Prop Dia. (ft. in.)	11 6.00	11 6.00	11 6.00	11 6.00	11 7.00	11 7.00	11 7.00

(1/72nd Scale in inches)

Wing Span	17.16	17.16	17.16	17.16	17.16	17.16	17.16
Wing Root Chord	3.16	3.16	3.16	3.16	3.16	3.16	3.16
Aileron Span	3.15	3.15	3.15	3.15	3.15	3.15	3.15
Flap Span	4.07	4.07	4.07	4.07	4.06	4.06	4.06
Length	11.46	11.46	11.31	11.31	12.30	12.46	12.46 12.39 *
Height	2.50	2.50	2.50	2.56	3.18	3.18	3.18
Horizontal Stabilizer Span	5.62	5.62	5.62	5.62	7.16	7.16	7.16
Horizontal Stabilizer Root Chord	1.85	1.84	1.84	1.84	1.86	1.86	1.86
MLG Track	3.49	3.49	3.52	3.52	3.52	3.52	3.52
MLG Dia.	0.76	0.76	0.76	0.76	0.76	0.76	0.77
Tailwheel Dia.	0.31	0.31	0.32	0.32	0.36	0.36	0.36
Prop Dia.	1.92	1.92	1.92	1.92	1.93	1.93	1.93

(1/48th Scale in inches)

Wing Span	25.95	25.95	25.95	25.95	25.95	25.95	25.95
Wing Root Chord	4.75	4.75	4.75	4.75	4.75	4.75	4.75
Aileron Span	4.73	4.73	4.73	4.73	4.73	4.73	4.73
Flap Span	6.11	6.11	6.11	6.11	6.10	6.10	6.10
Length	17.19	17.19	16.96	16.96	18.45	18.68	18.68 18.58 *
Height	3.75	3.75	3.75	3.84	4.77	4.77	4.77
Horizontal Stabilizer Span	8.44	8.44	8.44	8.44	10.75	10.75	10.75
Horizontal Stabilizer Root Chord	2.77	2.77	2.77	2.77	2.80	2.80	2.80
MLG Track	5.23	5.23	5.28	5.28	5.28	5.28	5.28
MLG Dia.	1.15	1.15	1.15	1.15	1.15	1.15	1.16
Tailwheel Dia.	0.46	0.46	0.48	0.48	0.54	0.54	0.54
Prop Dia.	2.87	2.87	2.87	2.87	2.89	2.89	2.89

*Cheyenne tail turret accounts for decrease in overall length of the B-17G.

PERFORMANCE CHARACTERISTICS AND TECHNICAL DATA

Model U.S. Army (Boeing)	Speed (MPH)			Time to Climb* (Min./Alt.)	Service Ceiling (Ft.)	Specific Range (Mi./MPH/Alt.)*			Weight (Pounds)*			Runway Length(Ft)*		Fuel Cap. (Gal.)	Oil Cap (Gal.)	Bomb Load (Qty-Wt)	Guns (Qty-Cal.)
	Max	Cruise	Landing			Ferry	Normal	Design	Ferry	Normal	Design	T.O.**	Land**				
"XB-17" (299)	236	140@ 70% Power	61.4@ 27,328#	8.25/10,000	24,620		3,011				34,432	2,200	2,200	1,700	152	8-600 (Max)	5-.30 or 5-.50
Y1B-17 (299B)	256@ 14,000	175@ Max Range Power	68	6.5/10,000	30,600	3400/178/10,000	2400/178/10,000	1300/178/10,000	43,650	42,500	34,873	1,515	3,400	1,700	180	8-600 (Max)	5-.30 or 5-.50
YB-17A (299F)	295@ 25,000	183@ 10,000	68	7.8/10,000	38,000	3600/176/10,000	2400/230/25,000	1300/230/25,000	45,650	44,500	37,000	1,700	2,500	1,700	180	8-600 (Max)	5-.30 or 5-.50
B-17B (299M)	292@ 25,000		68	7.0/10,000	36,000	3600/176/10,000	2400/230/25,000	1300/230/25,000	46,650	45,500	38,000	1,775	2,500	2,482	180	4-1,100 or 20-100	1-.30 & 6-.50
B-17C (299H)	323@ 25,000	227@ Max Range Power	68	7.5/10,000	37,000	3400/180/10,000	2000/250/25,000	625/245/25,000	49,650	48,500	38,320	1,850	2,700	2,492	180	8-600, 4-1,100 or 20-100	1-.30 and 6-.50
B-17D (299H)	323@ 25,000	227 Max Range Power	68	7.5/10,000	37,000	3400/180/10,000	2000/250/25,000	625/245/25,000	49,650	48,500	38,320	1,850	2,700	2,492	180	8-600, 4-1,100 or 20-100	1-.30 and 6-.50
B-17E (299-0)	317@ 25,000	226@ 15,000	70	7.1/10,000	36,000	3200/180/10,000	2000/224/15,000	550/250/25,500	53,000	51,000	40,260	2,150	2,700	2,490	180	4-1000, 20-100, 14-300	1-.30 & 8-.50
B-17F-1 thru -75 (BO) -20 (DL) -25 (VE)	325@ 25,000	160@ 5,000	73	25.7/20,000	37,500	2800/152/10,000	1300/200/10,000	240/250/25,000	56,500	56,500	40,437	3,400	2,900	2,520	147.6	8-1,000 or any comb. to 24-100	11-.50
B-17F-80 thru -130 (BO) -25 thru -65 (DL) -30 thru -50 (VE) (299-0)	325@ 25,000	160@ 5,000	73	25.7/20,000	37,500	3800/165/10,000	2200/200/10,000		65,500	65,500	48,726	3,400	2,900	3,630	147.6	8-1,000 or any comb to 24-100	11-.50
B-17G (299-0)	302@ 25,000	160	73	37.0/20,000	35,600	3400/180/10,000	2000/182/10,000		65,500	65,500	48,726	3,400	2,900	3,630	150	6-1,600 & 2-4,000	12-.50

* At design weight (B-17F/G at 55,000#)
** Runway length required for 50' obstacle clearance.
*** Flaps down.

- Sources: Boeing charts and U.S. Army.

MODELER'S SECTION

KIT REVIEWS

Entex 1/200th Scale B-17F

This very small kit has but a few pieces, but is accurate and takes just a few minutes to assemble. It fits in the smallest nook or cranny of your modeling shelf. We recommend this kit.

Crown 1/144th Scale B-17

This small kit is relatively accurate save for the shape of the cockpit which can be fixed with a little filing. It has few parts, and goes together quite nicely. We recommend this kit.

Lindberg 1/66th Scale B-17G

This is an older kit, and like Airfix and Revell, shows its age. It does not look right next to a 1/72nd kit due to its odd scale. Its accuracy is questionable too, with a wide variety of small, but noticeable errors. It has been recently reissued, but still may be a bit hard to come by in some areas. Except for collectors, we recommend staying with the better 1/72nd scale kits that are available.

Rareplanes 1/72nd Scale Y1B-17 and B-17C/D

This kit is typical of Rareplanes quality and is currently the only way a model can be built of an early version of the B-17. The Y1B-17 is a complete kit in itself, while the B-17C/D is just a fuselage. The wings have to be robbed from another kit. Use of the wings from one of the Hasegawa kits is recommended, and although this is expensive, it is the most accurate. There are a few minor faults with the kits, namely that the lower windows behind the bomb aimer's panel and those for the radio compartment are slightly mis-located. Also the intakes on top of the nacelles of the Y1B-17 need to be cleaned up. The fuselage-wing seam on the Y1B-17 is not the best, however it is minor considering the fact that this is a vac-u-form kit. We recommend this kit.

Rareplanes kit built as a B-17B. **(Lloyd)**

Frog 1/72nd Scale B-17E

This kit is quite a disappointment. It has a lot of problems that have to be eliminated to make it a presentable model. The aft fuselage is slightly too long, the waist windows are too small, the tail is shaped wrong, and the forward crew hatch is located on the wrong side of the fuselage. All window areas need to be filed out so that the clear parts fit. The propellers and landing gear should be replaced with those from the Airfix or Revell kits. Once the model has been finished, it looks pretty good, but it takes a lot of work to get it there. Since Frog is no longer in business this kit may become a collector's item in the near future.

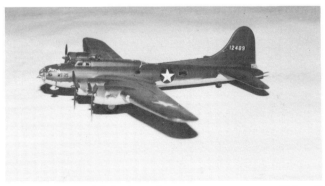

Frog B-17 in 1/72nd scale. **(Lloyd)**

Airfix 1/72nd Scale B-17G

The Airfix kit of the B-17 is one of their first kits, and as such shows its age. The model is reasonably accurate but has a number of faults that are very difficult to remedy. The shape of the nose is too flat, since it does not have the right taper, which makes the chin turret hang down too far. The clear nose piece is too rounded and does not fit well. The cockpit deck is too high and the top turret also sits too high. The wings have trailing edges that are much too thick, and the nacelle diameter is much too large. The shape of the vertical tail is slightly off, and the tail turret is inaccurate. The stabilizers also suffer from thick trailing edges. The kit as boxed from Airfix has always been marked as "A Bit O' Lace", and the decals were pretty good except that the girl's dress should be red instead of white. Also for this airplane the waist windows should not be staggered. The box art was somewhat misleading as to the color scheme: i.e. purple control surfaces! Surface detail on the kit is of the raised rivet variety, and being too large, the rivets should be removed. The kit was reboxed by MPC and offered a variety of markings which were of dubious quality and accuracy. There is really no way that the outline deficiencies of this kit can be corrected without a great deal of effort. It would be easier to buy the Hasegawa kit and save this kit for spare parts.

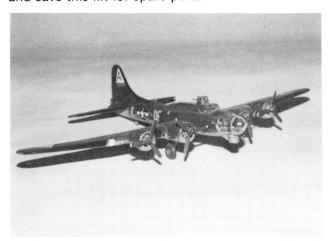

Airfix 1/72nd scale B-17G. **(Lloyd)**

Revell 1/72nd Scale B-17E/F

The Revell kit appeared about the same time as the Airfix kit, and as such, shows its age. The windscreen is too flat, as is the top fuselage deck. The rest of the fuselage is reasonably accurate but some work is needed in adding windows to the nose and above the cockpit since all that is provided are recesses molded into the plastic to accept the clear pieces. The wings suffer the same faults as the Airfix

Revell 1/72nd scale B-17. **(Lloyd)**

kit; notably oversize nacelles and thick trailing edges. The cowlings on the Revell kit have too large an opening. The cooling air slots on top of the wings are too large and too far aft. And rivets! They have to go. There is little interior to speak of, but it is not too important as it is very difficult to see anything through the clear plastic parts provided. The kit as originally produced was of the "F" series Fortress, and later on in production of the kit Revell added a different clear nose and called it an "E". Unfortunately that is all that they did. There were a few noticeable changes in the two aircraft: the "E" had narrow chord propellors, the "F" had the "paddle blade" props. The early "E" birds had a remotely controlled Bendix turret that was eventually replaced by the Sperry manned turret. Both Revell kits have the Sperry turret. Revell originally boxed their kit as the "Memphis Belle", and later was reboxed with markings for the "Lady Luck". When Revell modified the molds, the markings were for the "Peggy D" in Revell USA kits and an RAF Coastal Command aircraft in Revell UK kits. The markings in all of the kits were of mediocre quality save for the Revell UK release, which were pretty good. The same recommendation for the Airfix kit holds for the Revell kit - save it for spares and use the Hasegawa kits.

Matchbox 1/72nd Scale B-17G

Matchbox's new B-17G was received with mixed feelings. The panel lines are sparse, but reasonably accurate, and most are raised and appear quite crisp. Gone are the trenches found in their previous kits. In general the outline of the individual pieces is quite accurate.

The clear parts are the greatest disappointment. They have a bubble-like appearance with no crisp edges. The radio compartment side windows are a bit too large, and no framing details are present on the nose glazing. The apex of the nose glazing is a bit too high. The ball turret is split fore and aft, installs in an awkward manner, and is extended too far for an airplane on the ground. The ball turret is actually molded as a clear cylinder with a spherical bottom.

The forward fuselage is assembled as a separate unit. The windows appear to be reasonably accurate although the cheek gun fairings are a bit short in the vertical dimension. Interior detail consists of two bulkheads, a floor, two seats, a pair of tall control columns, and a top turret base in the cockit. As with all of the other B-17G kits to date, the waist gun windows are staggered.

A unique feature is the optional tail gun. Both the Boeing standard tail gun installation and the Cheynne turret have been provided. The ball for the Cheynne turret is too small in diameter as it should fair smoothly into the fuselage tail cone, and not fit like a button. The modeler is faced with the decision of building a version with the old tail gun position or having to modify the Cheynne ball.

Door and hatch outlines are deep groves. All hinge and latch detail is lacking. The ADF "football" antenna is too big, too deep, and has too much fairing into the mast. The air inlets in the wing leading edges, though accurately placed, are a bit too small.

Some frontal detail is contained in the engine pieces. However, the cowlings detract from the model in that they are about ⅛th inch too short, and the loss is found in the abbreviated cowl flaps. The supercharger exhaust manifolds appear to be too large in diameter. The exhaust housings for the supercharger turbines are too rounded. However, the turbine wheel and exhaust vane details are reasonably captured.

Details on the main landing gear struts are reasonable, though sparse. No tire tread or wheel hub detail has been included. The tail wheel installation (wheel, strut, and fuselage well) appear to be a bit large. The addition of a boot within the wheel well would help obscure the large gaping hole.

The overall appearance of the assembled kit leaves a bit to be desired. It is there, but it lacks the crispness in detail needed to make it an outstanding kit. To build a bare metal bird from this kit would be a mistake. A good camouflage paint scheme, especially one in which the consistant paint pattern is broken, can result in a reasonable model.

Markings for three B-17Gs are provided in the kit. 1. B-17G-30-DL, serial number 42-38201 (tail number 238201), "2nd Patches", operated by the 346th BS, 99th BG, 15th AF, with staggered waist windows and the standard Boeing tail turret may be built in a camouflaged scheme with bare metal patches to break up the paint scheme. 2. Another set of markings are for B-17G-35-DL, serial number 42-107027 (tail number 2107027), "Hikin' for Home", operated by the 322nd BS, 91st BG, 8th AF. 3. The third airplane "Kwiturbitchin" appears to have an erroneous tail number for any B-17! With the better Hasegawa kits available, it is difficult to recommend the Matchbox kit.

Hasegawa 1/72nd scale B-17F. **(Lloyd)**

Hasegawa 1/72nd Scale B-17F and B-17G

The newest of the 1/72nd B-17 kits are from Hasegawa and are the best. Both kits are quite accurate, with a minimum of faults. The fit of the parts is quite good, and only a minimum of putty is needed to fill some very small seam lines. The rest can be taken care of with some light sanding. The only thing that can be faulted on either kit is that the forward entry hatch is scribed slightly too large and the windscreen scribing is wrong--the top of the windscreen should be parallel to the center line. A fault on the "G" kit is that the tail gunner's canopy is not deep

Hasegawa B-17G with modifications. **(Lloyd)**

enough, which is a minor fault, but it does show. The wingtip vents on the "F" kit have to be filled in, and the interior is rather sparse. The trailing edges are all thin, which is a nice feature not seen on any of the other B-17 kits so far. The decals are of excellent quality, but the "G" kit cannot be built out of the box with the kit decals. The markings are for a B-17G with unstaggered waist windows, but the kit windows are staggered. Overall, this is the best model of the B-17 that is available, and we highly recommend it.

Monogram 1/48th Scale B-17G

The kit is representative of the early "G" being molded with the unstaggered waist windows and the early tail turret. As is usual with Monogram, there is a great amount of interior detail which is nicely done. The problem is that there is no bomb bay detail and it takes quite a bit of effort to detail this area if you want to open the bomb bay. The kit is accurate in outline, and the fit of the parts is good. The underside of the wing-fuselage joint does not match very well, although this is not too noticeable. All of the intakes in the leading edge of the wings need to be modified so that they look like intakes and not like holes in the wings. The trailing edges seem to be slightly thick, even for this scale. The fabric on the control surfaces is slightly overdone and needs to be sanded down. With a little work, this kit can be modified into the later versions with staggered waist windows and the Cheyenne turret. A version of this kit is also available with a clear fuselage half that permits viewing of the interior. Overall this

is an excellent kit and we recommend it.

Revell 1/48th Scale B-17F

If you remove the chin turret, throw away most of the interior, change the decals, add external bomb racks, change the color of the plastic, and "internationalize" the instructions from the Monogram kit, you will have a Revell kit. There are only a few minor changes in molding certain parts to complete the difference in the two kits. All the major components fit each other exactly!! Most of the same things said about the Monogram kit hold for the Revell kit, save for the interior. All you get with the Revell kit is the cockpit area, and even that has been simplified. The two main advantages to the Revell kit is that it is an "F" variant (which leads to possibilities to making earlier versions of the B-17), and the price which is a few dollars less than the Monogram kit. We recommend this kit.

Revell 1/48th scale B-17F.   **(Revell)**

PLACE OF HONOR: This Hasegawa 1/72nd scale B-17G by Jamie Pye won the Detail & Scale Special Award for the best detailed aircraft model in the 1981 IPMS/USA National Convention in New York City. The model had a complete scratchbuilt interior from nose to tail.   **(Pye)**

DECALS

1/72nd DECALS

NAME	S/N	TYPE	AF	AD	WG	GP	SQ	CODE	DECAL SOURCE
A Bit O' Lace	42-97976	B-17G-40-VE	8	3	4	447	-	D	Airfix & Hasegawa Kits
Chow Hound	42-31367	B-17G-15-BO	8	1	1	91	322	LG-R	Hasegawa Kit
Delta Rebel No. 2	42-5077	B-17F-30-BO	8	1	1	91	323	OR-T	Microscale 72-23 & ESCI
Eight Ball	42-3138	B-17F-25-DL	8	1	1	91	323	OR-H	Microscale 72-23
Elusive Elcy	42-5888	B-17F-40-VE	8	3	4	94	331	QE-	ESCI
General Ike	42-97061	B-17G-40-BO	8	1	1	91	401	LL-B	ESCI
Hell's Angel's	41-24577	B-17F-25-BO	8	1	1	303	358	VK-D	Hasegawa Kit
Hikin' For Home	42-107027	B-17G-35-DL	8	1	1	91	322	LG-Y	Matchbox Kit & Microscale 72-182
Just Plain Lonesome	42-39975	B-17G-10-VE	8	1	1	91	324	DF-Z	ESCI
Knockout Dropper	41-24605	B-17F-27-BO	8	1	1	303	359	BN-R	Microscale 72-23*
Kwiturbitchin	44-46544	B-17G-55-DL	15	-	5	97	414	4	Matchbox kit
Lady Luck	42-29837	B-17F-75-BO	8	1	1	91	324	DF-A	Revell Kit
Little Miss Mischief	42-97880	B-17G-35-VE	8	1	1	91	-	-	US Airfix Kit
Marnita No. 2 Thunderbird	42-5724	B-17F-5-VE	8	1	1	91	322	LG-T	Microscale 72-281
Memphis Belle	41-24485	B-17F-10-BO	8	1	1	91	324	DF-A	Minicraft Kit, Revell Kit, & Microscale 72-23
Mount 'N' Ride	42-31585	B-17G-20-BO	8	1	1	91	323	OR-B	Detail & Scale 0172
Nine-O-Nine	42-31909	B-17G-30-BO	8	1	1	91	323	OR-R	Minicraft Kit
Ole' Doodle Bug	43-38625	B-17G-90-BO	8	3	93	385		X	Minicraft Kit
Peggy D	41-9043	B-17E	8	-	1	97	342	-	Revell Kit & ESCI
Pistol Packin' Mama	42-37779	B-17G-10-DL	8	1	1	91	324	DF-B	ESCI
Priority Gal	42-97304	B-17G-45-BO	8	1	1	91	323	OR-C	Microscale 72-182
2nd Patches	42-38201	B-17G-30-DL	15	-	5	99	346	-	Matchbox Kit
Suzy Q	41-2489	B-17E	5	-	-	19	93	-	Frog Kit
Target for Tonite	41-24615	B-17F-27-BO	8	1	40	305	422	JJ-F	Detail & Scale 0172
The Village Flirt	42-29739	B-17F-70-BO	8	1	1	91	323	OR-M	Detail & Scale 0172
The Eagle's Wrath	41-24524	B-17F-20-BO	8	1	1	91	323	OR-O	ESCI
The Witche's Tit	42-5382	B-17F-50-BO	8	1	1	91	323	OR-B	ESCI & Microscale 72-23
Time's-A-Wastin'	42-102504	B-17G-50-BO	8	1	1	91	401	LL-D	Microscale 72-182
Vicious Virgin	42-5341	B-17F-45-BO	8	1	40	303	427	GN-Q	Microscale 72-23
None	36-151	YB-17	-	-	-	2	49	BB 80	Microscale 72-182
None	None	B-17F	RAF COASTAL COMMAND						Revell of England Kit

*Individual aircraft letters changed due to aircraft losses within any given unit. This aircraft carried both BN-A and BN-R codes.

1/48th DECALS

NAME	S/N	TYPE	AF	AD	WG	GP	SQ	CODE	DECAL SOURCE
A Bit O' Lace	42-97976	B-17G-40-VE	8	3	4	447		D	Microscale 48-21
Chowhound	42-31367	B-17G-15-BO	8	1	1	91	322	LG-R	Monogram Kit
Eight Ball	42-3138	B-17F-25-DL	8	1	1	91	323	OR-H	Microscale 48-59*
El Lobo	42-32101	B-17G-35-BO	8	1	94	457	748	F	Monogram Kit
Hell's Angel's	42-24577	B-17F-25-BO	8	1	1	303	358	VK-D	Microscale 48-59*
Joker	42-31684	B-17G-25-BO	15	-	5	463	-	-	Microscale 48-17
Little Miss Mischief	42-97880	B-17G-35-VE	8	1	1	91	-	-	Microscale 48-17
Little Patches	42-31578	B-17G-20-BO	8	1	1	91	401	LL-L	Microscale 48-59*
Memphis Belle	42-24485	B-17F-10-BO	8	1	1	91	324	DF-A	Revell Kit
Nine-O-Nine	42-31909	B-17G-30-BO	8	1	1	91	323	OR-R	Microscale 48-17
Shoo Shoo Shoo Baby	42-32078	B-17G-35-BO	8	1	1	91	401	LL-E	Monogram Visible B-17 Kit
The Witch's Tit	42-5382	B-17F-50-BO	8	1	1	91	323	OR-B	Microscale 48-59
Thunderbird	42-38050	B-17G-25-DL	8	1	40	303	359	BN-U	Monogram Visible B-17 Kit
Wabash Cannonball	42-29947	B-17F-75-BO	8	1	1	91	322	LG-U	Microscale 48-21
(Nude riding cloud on fin)	42-97719	B-17G-30-VE	15	-	5	463	-	-	Microscale 48-21

*S/N not included on decal sheet.

AF - Air Force, AD - Air Division, WG-Wing, GP-Group, SQ-Squadron

B-17F-70-BO, "The Village Flirt" in flight. *(P.G. Mack)*

Detail & Scale's first decal sheet in 1/72nd scale (DS-0172) is entitled, "Sexy B-17s." Included are two B-17Fs and a B-17G, all with fancy ladies for nose art. In addition to the specific markings for each aircraft, the sheet includes prop stenciling, fuel filler cap markings, instrument panels, and data blocks for each particular aircraft, "Target for Tonite," a B-17F-27-BO, 41-24615, belonged to the 8th Air Force, 1st Air Division, 305th Bomb Group, 422nd Bomb Squadron flying out of Chelveston, England. The pilot was Herbert J. Coleman. "The Village Flirt", a B-17F-70-BO, 42-29739 belonged to the 8th Air Force, 1st Air Division, 91st Bomb Group, 323rd Bomb Squadron our of Bassingbourn, England. The pilot was Philip G. Mack. The B-17G-20-BO is, "Mount' N Ride," 42-31585, and was from the same unit as "The Village Flirt". These decals are designed specifically for the Hasegawa B-17F and B-17G kits.

Nose art on "Target for Tonite", a B-17F-27-BO. Although this photo has faded with age, the mission markings and female with her garter belt and nylons are visible. *(Coleman)*

"Mount' N Ride", an OD and gray B-17G-20-BO. This photo comes from Joseph Harlick, the unit photographer. The artist for this aircraft was Anthony Starcer. *(J. Harlick)*

REFERENCE LISTING

Note: Listed here are references on the B-17 Flying Fortress that should prove helpful in providing information and photographs of a different nature and format than what is presented in this publication. There are many fine references on the B-17 Flying Fortress and they all cannot be listed here. The fact that a given reference is not included in this list is not intended to reflect unfavorably on that reference.

1. Air Combat Special - The Boeing B-17G, Air Combat Special No. 1, Rockaway, N.J., 1971.
2. Aircraft Year Book, Lancair Publishers, Inc., N.Y., Years 1939-1945, 1949, 1950 & 1951.
3. The American Heritage of Flight, American Heritage, N.Y., 1962.
4. Bailey, R. H., The Air War in Europe: 1940-1945, Time-Life Books, Inc., Chicago, 1979.
5. Bendiner, Elmer, The Fall of Fortress, G. P. Putnam's Sons N.Y., 1980.
6. Birdsall, S. B-17 in Action, Squadron/Signal Publications No. 12, Carrolton, Texas, 1973.
7.   "   The B-17 Flying Fortress, Arco Publishing Co., Inc, N.Y., 1965.
8.   "   Flying Buccaneers, Doubleday & Company, Inc., N.Y., 1977.
9.   "   Hell's Angels, Grenadier Books, Canoga Park, Ca., 1969.
10. Blakebrough, K., The Fireball Outfit - the 457th BG, Aero Publishers, Fallbrook, Ca., 1968.
11. Boeing B-17 Flying Fortress, Famous Airplanes of the World Koku Fan, No. 24, Bunrin-Do, Japan 1974.
12. Bowers, P.M., Boeing Aircraft Since 1916, Putnam, London, 1966.
13.   "   Fortress in the Sky, Sentry Books, Inc., Granada Hills, Ca., 1976.
14. Cadin, M., Air Force - A Pictorial History of American Airpower, Rinehart & Co., Inc., N.Y., 1957.
15.   "   Everything But The Flak, Duell, Sloan & Pearce, N.Y.
16.   "   Flying Forts, The B-17 in World War II, Meredith Press, N.Y., 1968.
17. Cristy, J., & Shamburger, B., Summon the Stars, A.S. Barnes & Co., Inc. Cranberry, N.J., 1970.
18. Collison, T., Flying Fortress, the Story of the Boeing Bomber, C. Scribner's Sons, N.Y., 1943.
19. Craven, W. F., & Cate, J. L., The Army Air Forces in World War II, University of Chicago Press, Chicago, 1948.
20. Fahey, J. C., U.S. Army Aircraft 1908-1946, Ships and Aircraft, N.Y., 1946.
21. Freeman, R., Boeing B-17G Flying Fortress, Vol. 205, Profile Publications, Ltd., Berkshire.
22.   "   B-17 Fortress at War, Ian Allan, Ltd., London, 1977.
23.   "   The Mighty Eighth, Doubleday & Co., Inc., N.Y., 1970.
24. Green, W., Famous Bombers of the Second World War, Vol. I, Hanover House, N.Y., 1959.
25. Goldberg, A., A History of the United States Air Force 1907-1957, D. van Nostrand, N.J., 1958.
26. Jablonski, E., Airwar, Vol. 1 & 2, Doubleday, N.Y., 1971.
27.   "   A Pictorial History of the World War II Years, Doubleday, N.Y., 1977.
28.   "   Flying Fortress, Doubleday, N.Y., 1965.
29. Jane's All the World's Aircraft, MacMillan, N.Y., Vols. 1939-1945.
30. Jones, L.S., U.S. Bombers B-1 - B-70, Aero Publishers, Fallbrook, California, 1962.
31.   "   U.S. Bombers - Army and Air Force - 1929-1980, Aero Publishers, Fallbrook, California, 1980.
32. Natly, B., & Berger, C., The Men Who Bombed the Third Reich, Elsevier-Dutton, N.Y., 1978.
33. Simon & Schuster Encyclopedia of World War II, The, Simon & Schuster, N.Y., 1978.
34. Siefring, T. A., U.S. Air Force in World War II, Chartwell Books, N.J., 1977.
35. Sunderman, J. F., World War II in the Air - Europe, Franklin Watts, N.Y., 1963.
36. World War II in the Air - The Pacific. Franklin Watts, N.Y., 1962.
37. Swanborough, G., & Bowers, P.M., United States Military Aircraft Since 1909, Putnam, London, 1963.
38.   "   United States Navy Aircraft Since 1911, Putnam, London, 1968 & 1976.
39. Thetford, O., Aircraft of the Royal Air Force Since 1918, Putnam, London, 1962.
40. Thompson, C. D., The Boeing B-17E & F Flying Fortress, No. 77, Profile Publications, Berkshire.
41. Wagner, R., American Combat Planes, Hanover House, N.Y., 1960.